Editor in Chief
Ina Massler Levin, M.A.

Editor
Eric Migliaccio

Contributing Editor
Sarah Smith

Creative Director
Karen J. Goldfluss, M.S. Ed.

Cover Design
Tony Carrillo / Marilyn Goldberg

Teacher Created Resources
12621 Western Avenue
Garden Grove, CA 92841
www.teachercreated.com
ISBN: 978-1-4206-5914-6

Reprinted, 2025 (PO605858)
Made in U.S.A.

Teacher Created Resources

This book belongs to

____

Ready·Set·Learn

Get Ready to Learn!

Get ready, get set, and go! Boost your child's learning with this exciting series of books. Geared to help children practice and master many needed skills, the *Ready·Set·Learn* books are bursting with 64 pages of learning fun. Use these books for . . .

- enrichment
- skills reinforcement
- extra practice

With their smaller size, the *Ready·Set·Learn* books fit easily in children's hands, backpacks, and book bags. All your child needs to get started are pencils, crayons, and colored pencils.

A full sheet of colorful stickers is included. Use these stickers for . . .

- decorating pages
- rewarding outstanding effort
- keeping track of completed pages

Celebrate your child's progress by using these stickers on the reward chart located on the inside cover. The blue-ribbon sticker fits perfectly on the certificate on page 64.

With *Ready·Set·Learn* and a little encouragement, your child will be on the fast track to learning fun!

Follow the Letters

Directions: Follow the letters of the alphabet to find the picture. Start at the star. Color the picture.

Dot-to-Dot Stars

Directions: Follow the stars in order from A to Z. What constellation do you see in the night sky? What animal do you see?

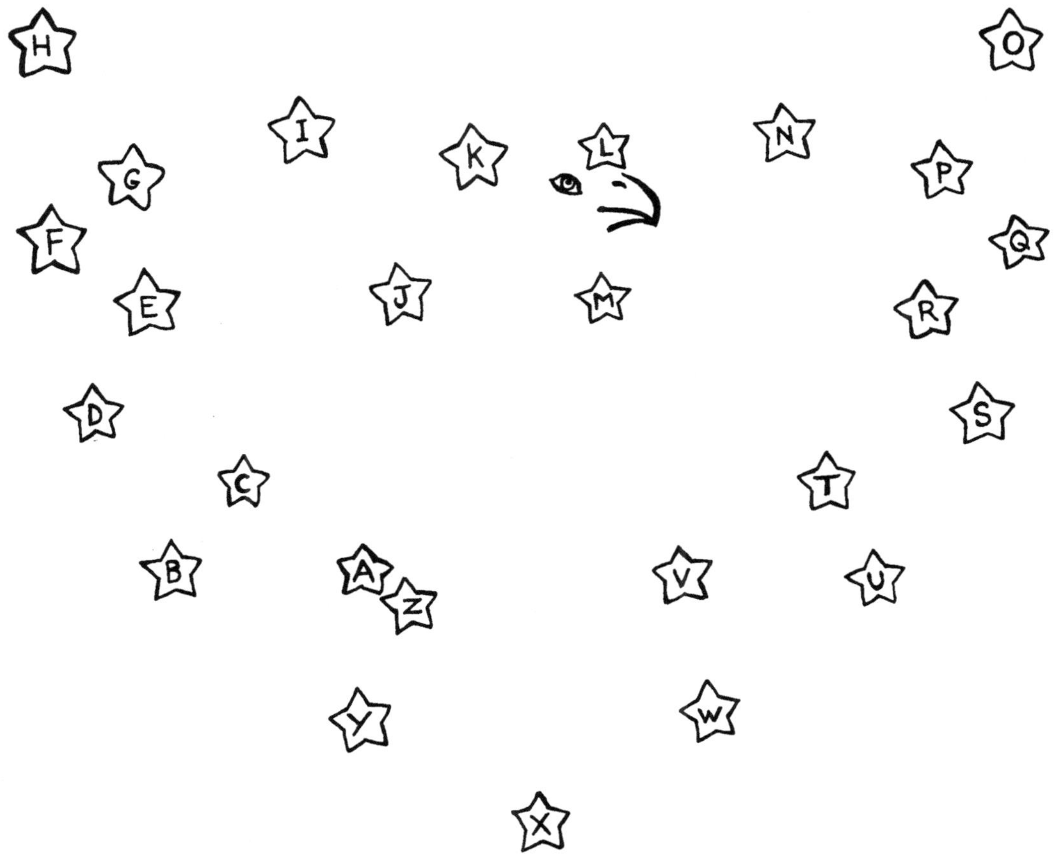

Backwards ABC

Directions: Follow the letters of the alphabet backwards to complete the picture. Start at the star. Color the picture.

Super Star

Directions: Follow the dots in an AB pattern to create a star. Begin at the top (A). Go in the direction of the arrow.

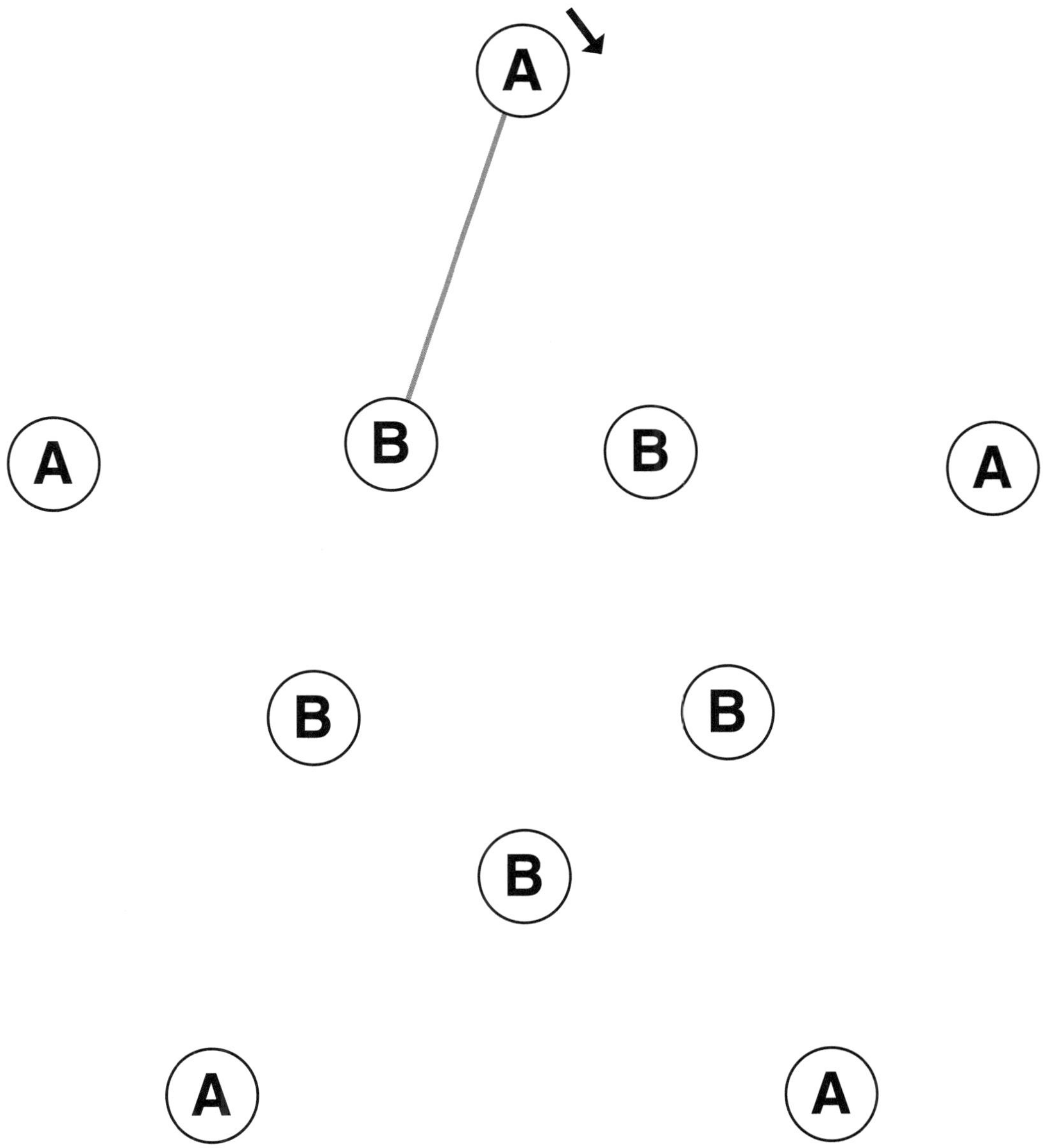

Joining the Dots to 20

Directions: Here is a hidden picture. What do you think it might be? Starting with the star at 0, join the numbers from 0 to 20 to complete the picture.

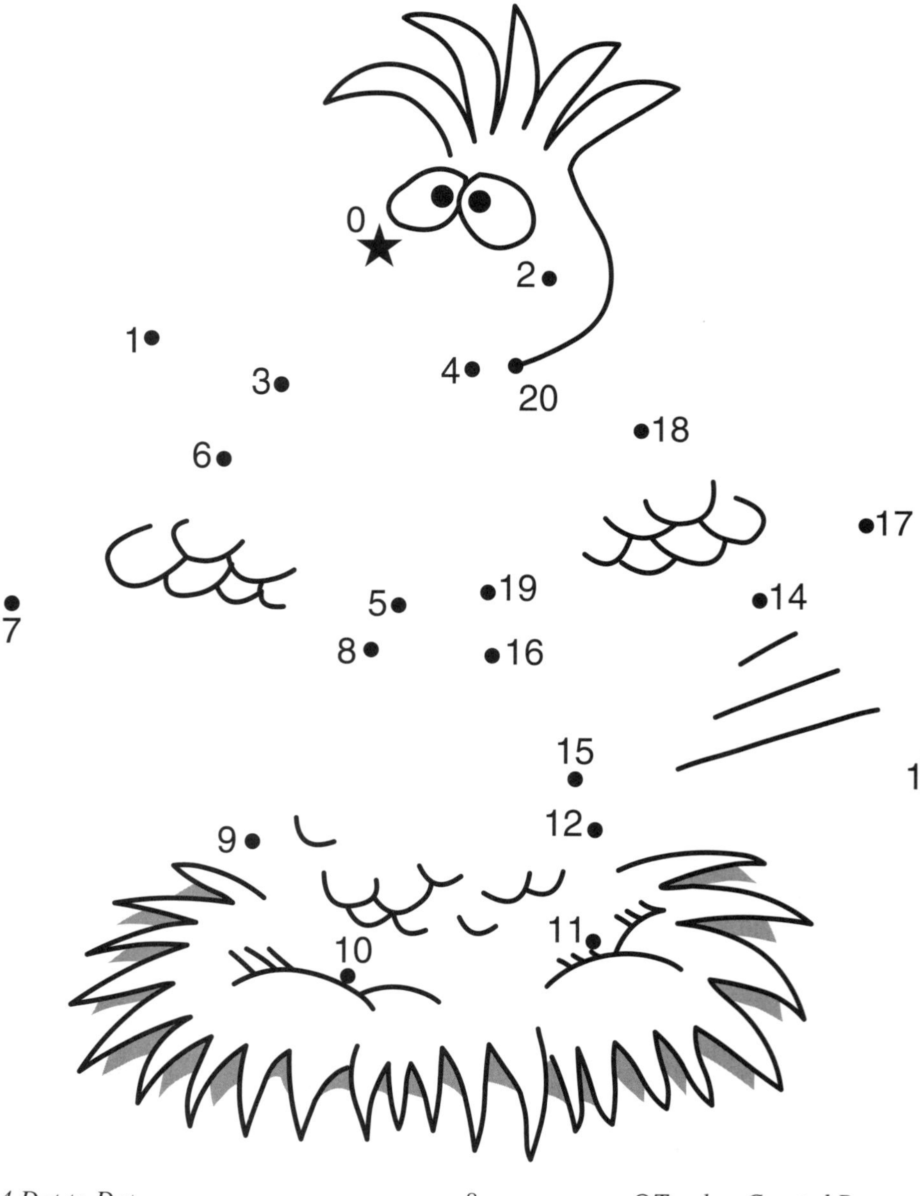

Rainy Day

Directions: Be careful with this double dot to dot. Connect the dots from 1 to 20, beginning at the star. Then connect the triangles from 1 to 14 to complete the picture.

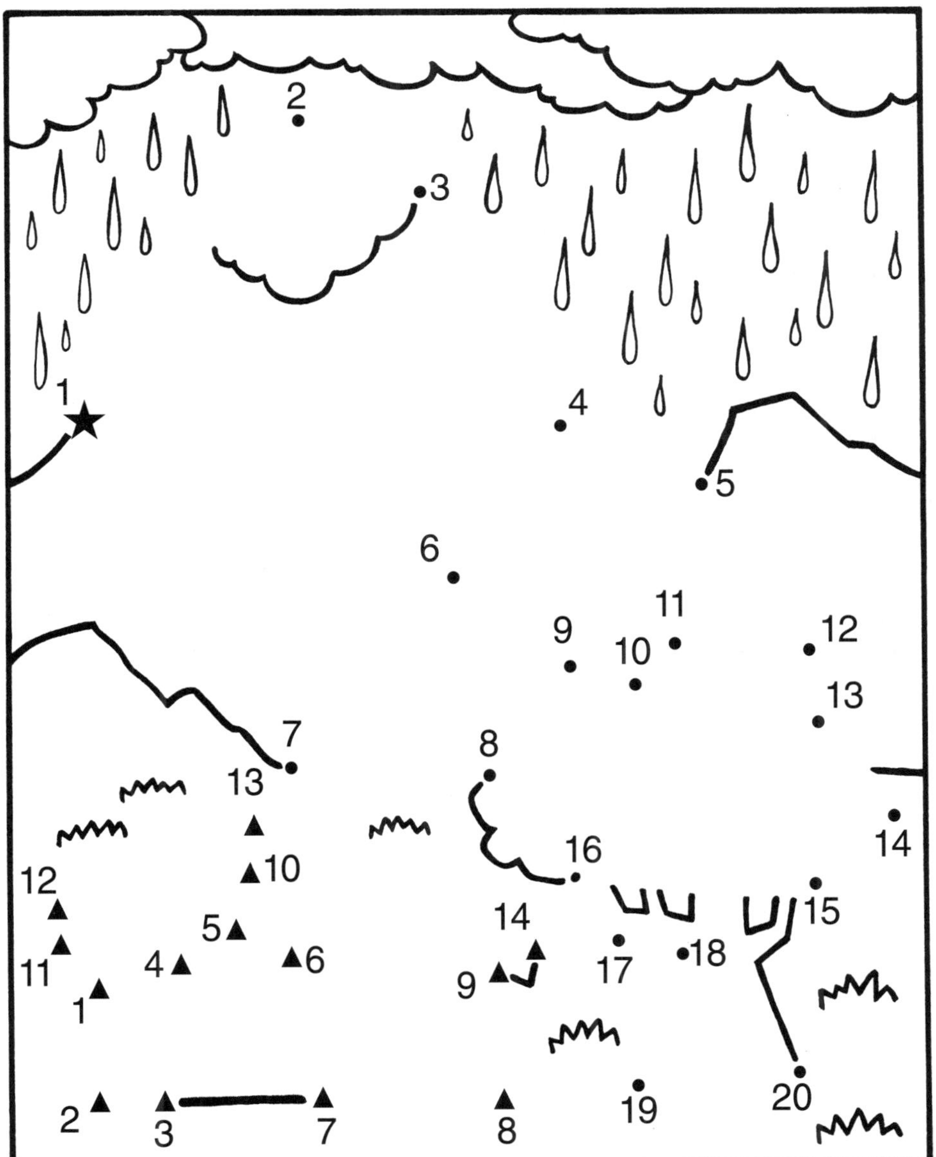

Join the Numbers

Direction: Join the dots from 1 to 20. Then join the triangles from 1 to 9.

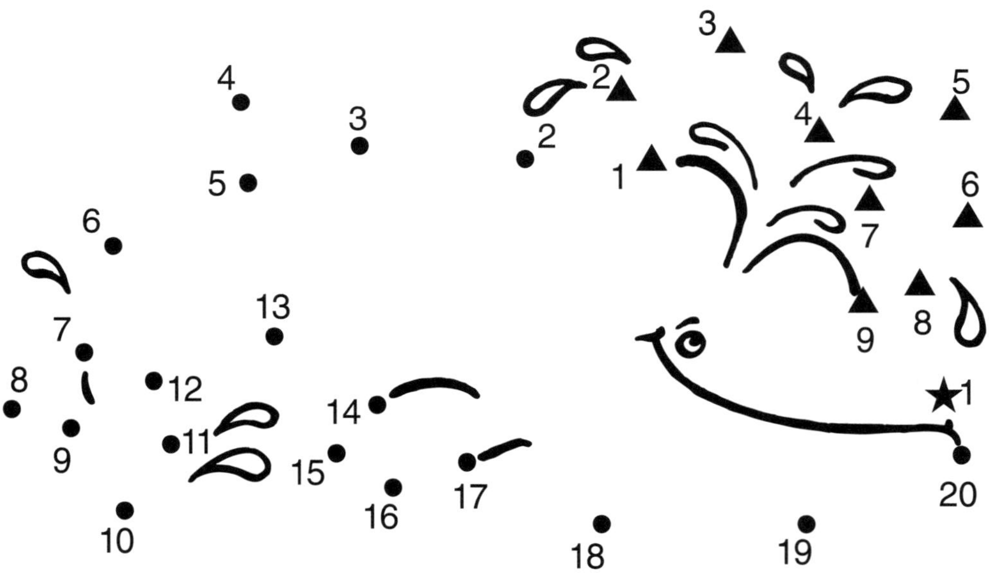

I am a ________________________.

Sunny Day

Directions: Connect the dots from 1 to 22 to complete the picture.

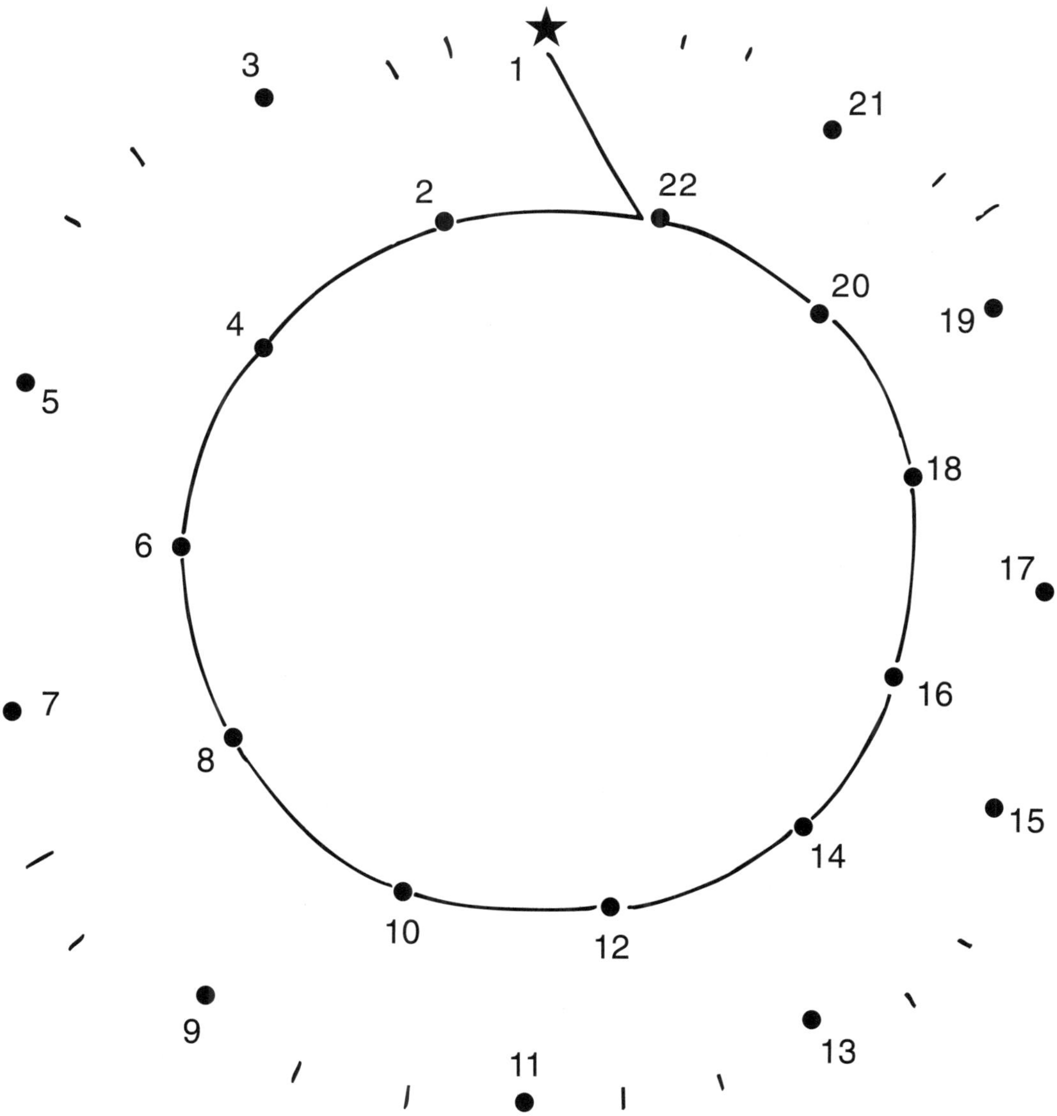

Lamb

Directions: Connect the dots from 1 to 25 to complete the picture.

Camel

Directions: Connect the dots from 1 to 27 to complete the picture.

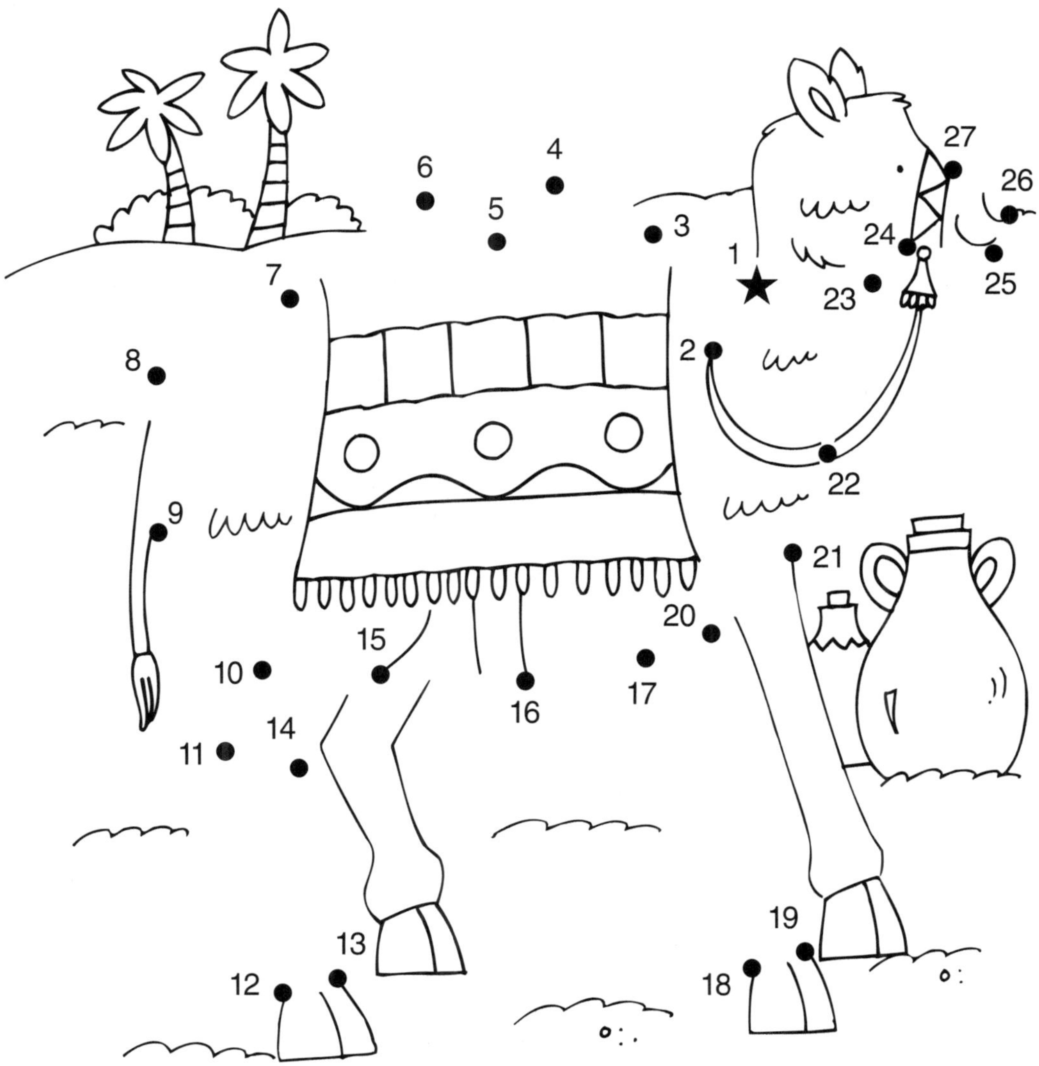

Pineapple

Directions: Connect the dots from 1 to 30 to complete the picture.

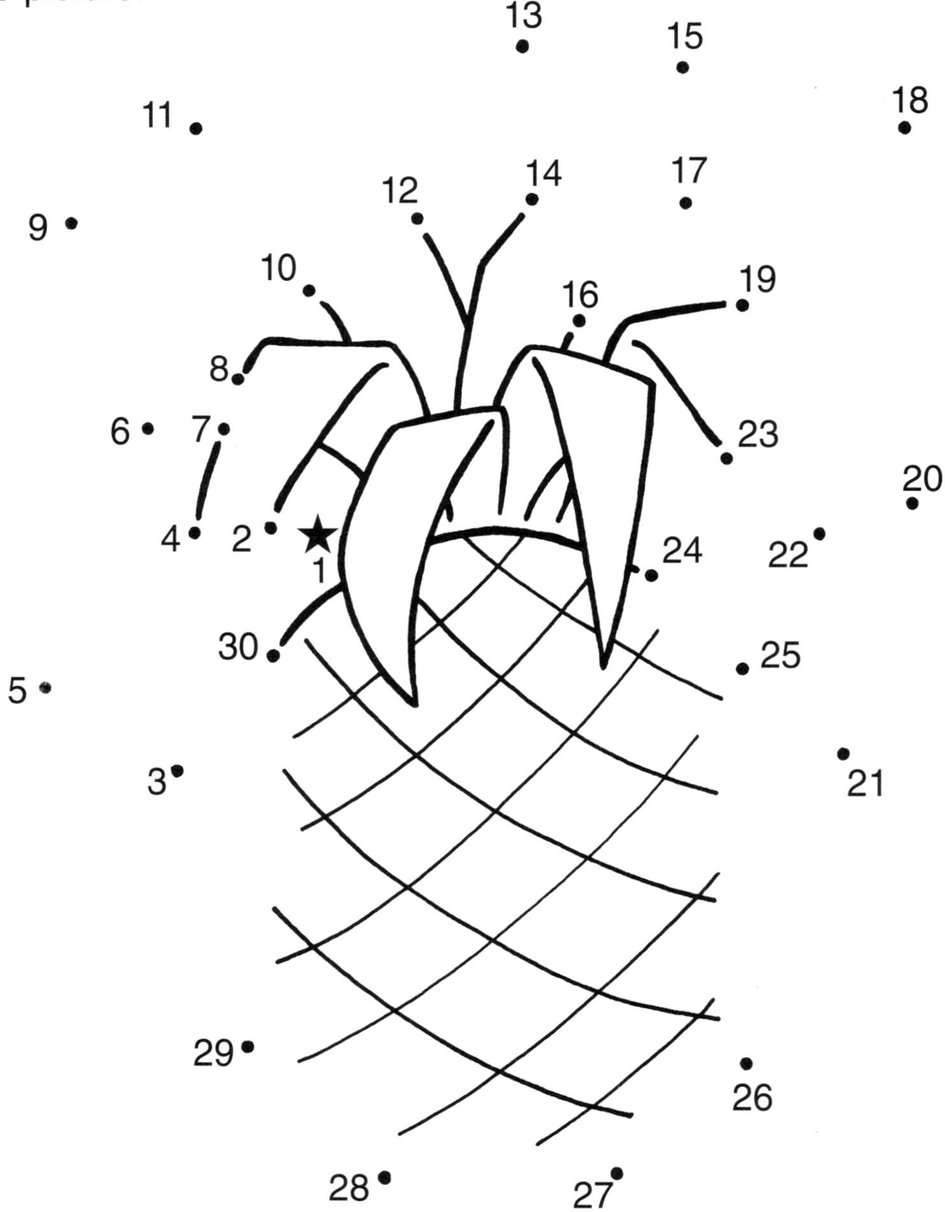

Snowman

Directions: Connect the dots from 1 to 30 to complete the picture.

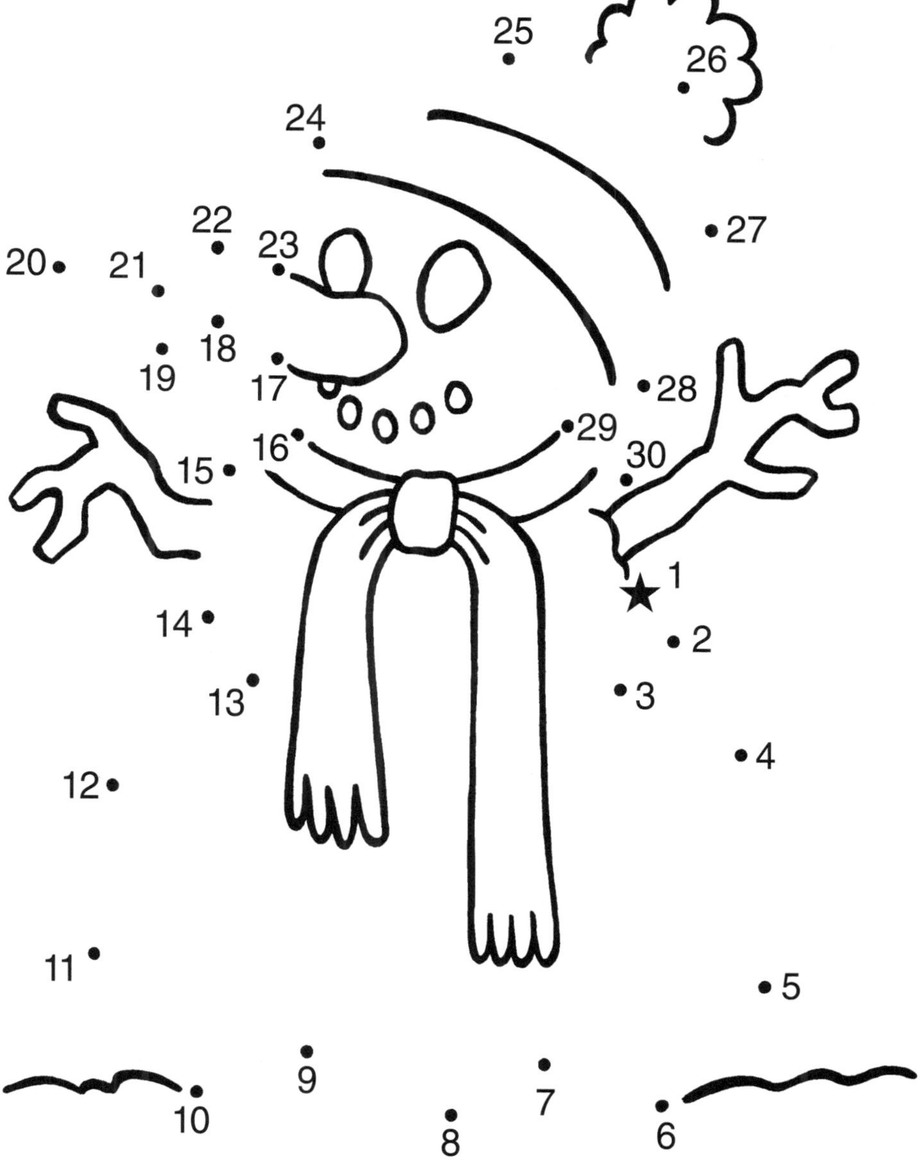

Time to Fish

Directions: Connect the dots from 1 to 31 to complete the picture.

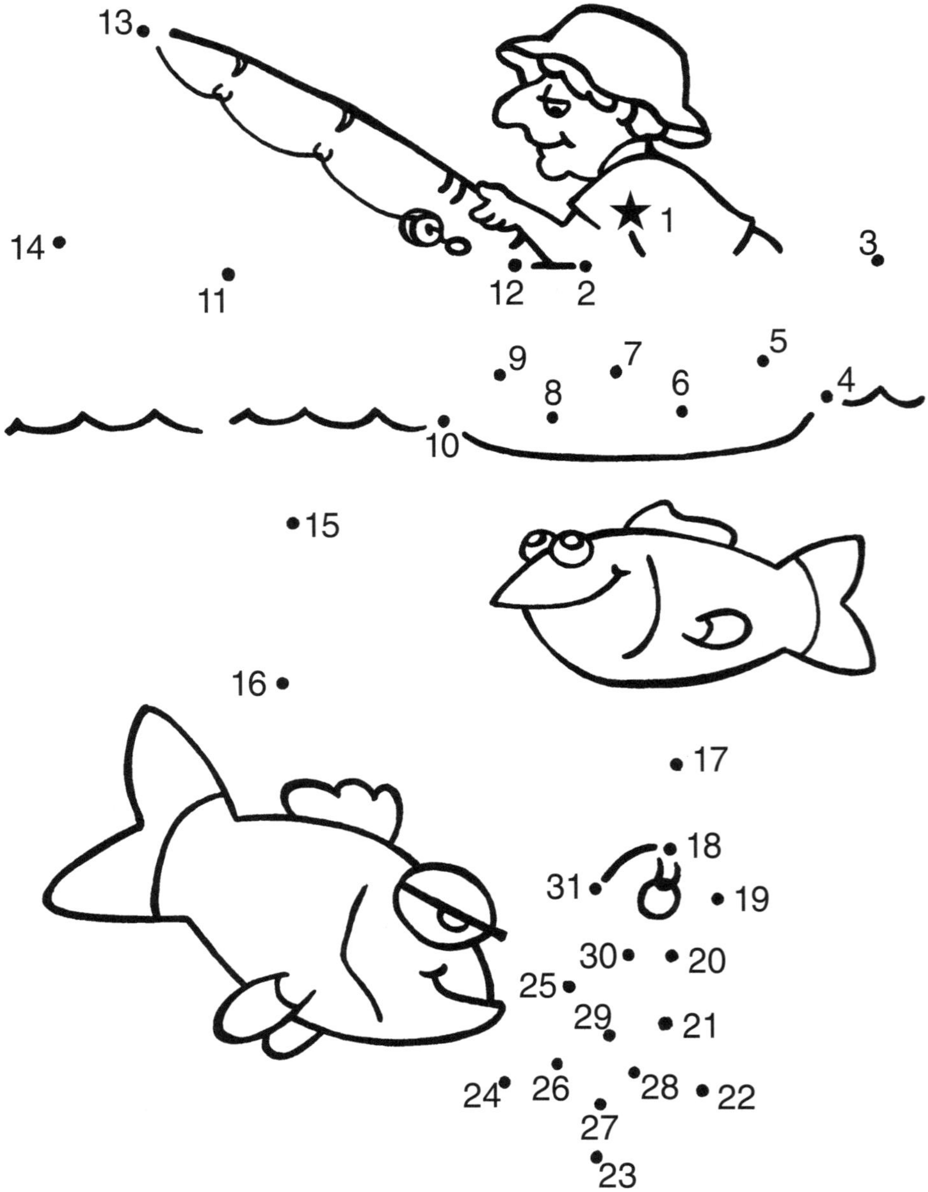

Grasshopper

Directions: Connect the dots from 1 to 32 to complete the picture.

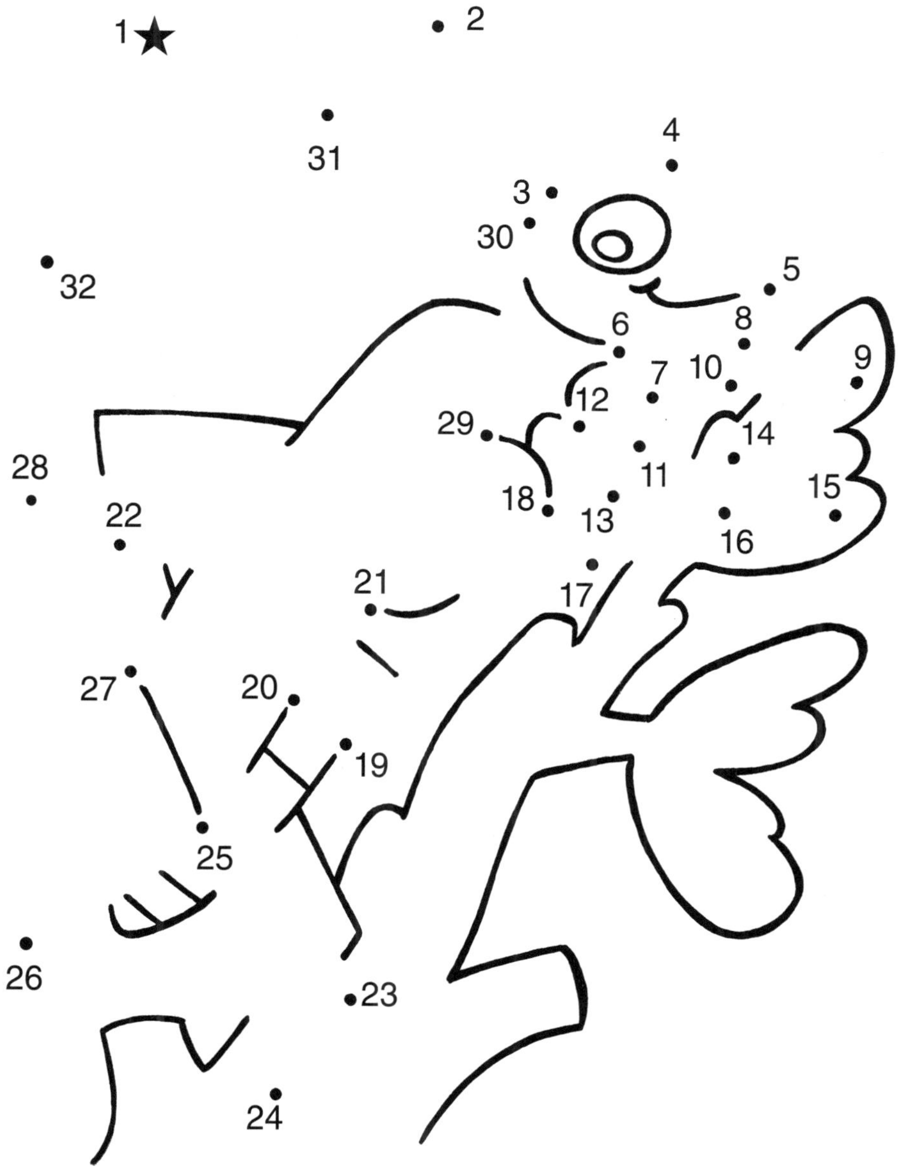

Rocket

Directions: Connect the dots from 1 to 33 to complete the picture.

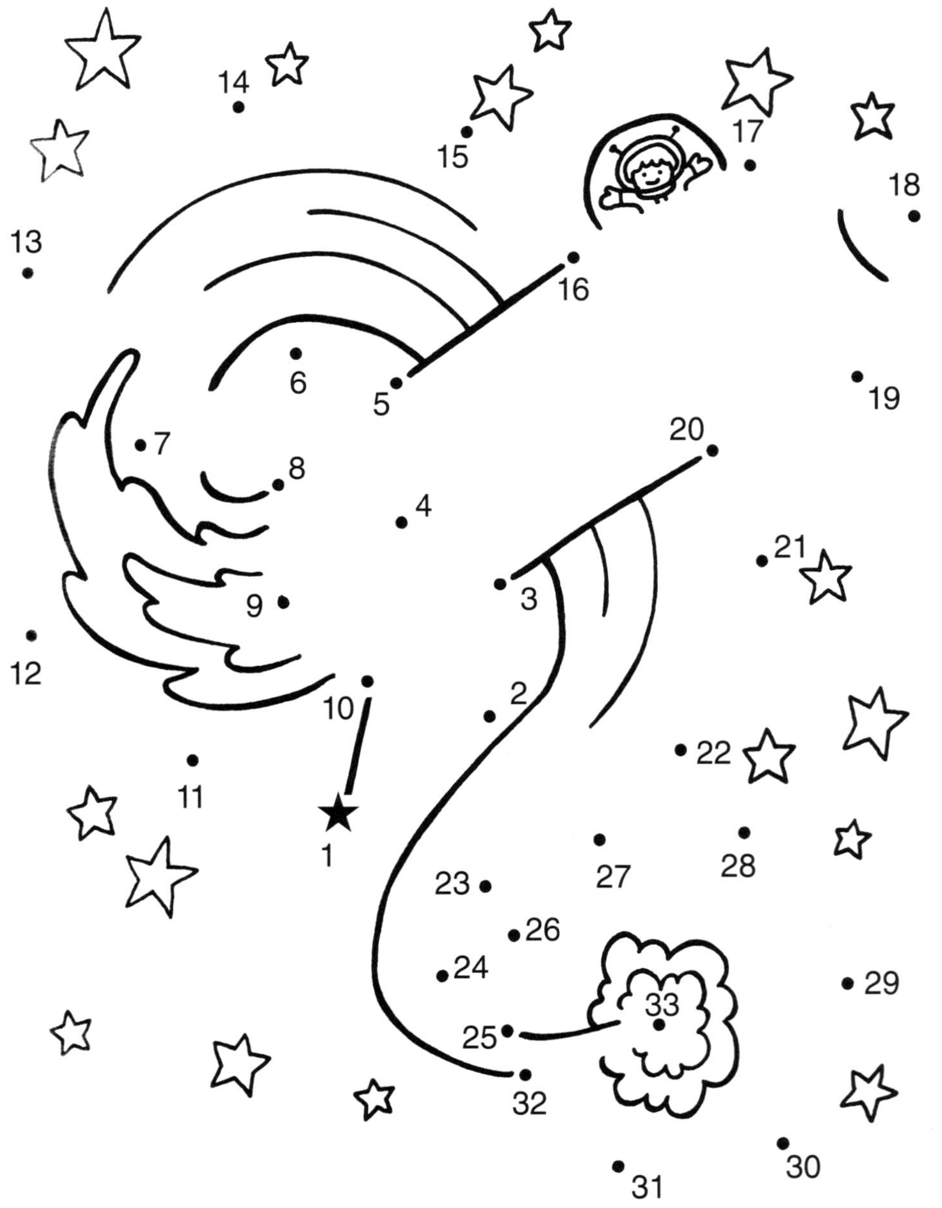

Elephant

Directions: Connect the dots from 1 to 34 to complete the picture.

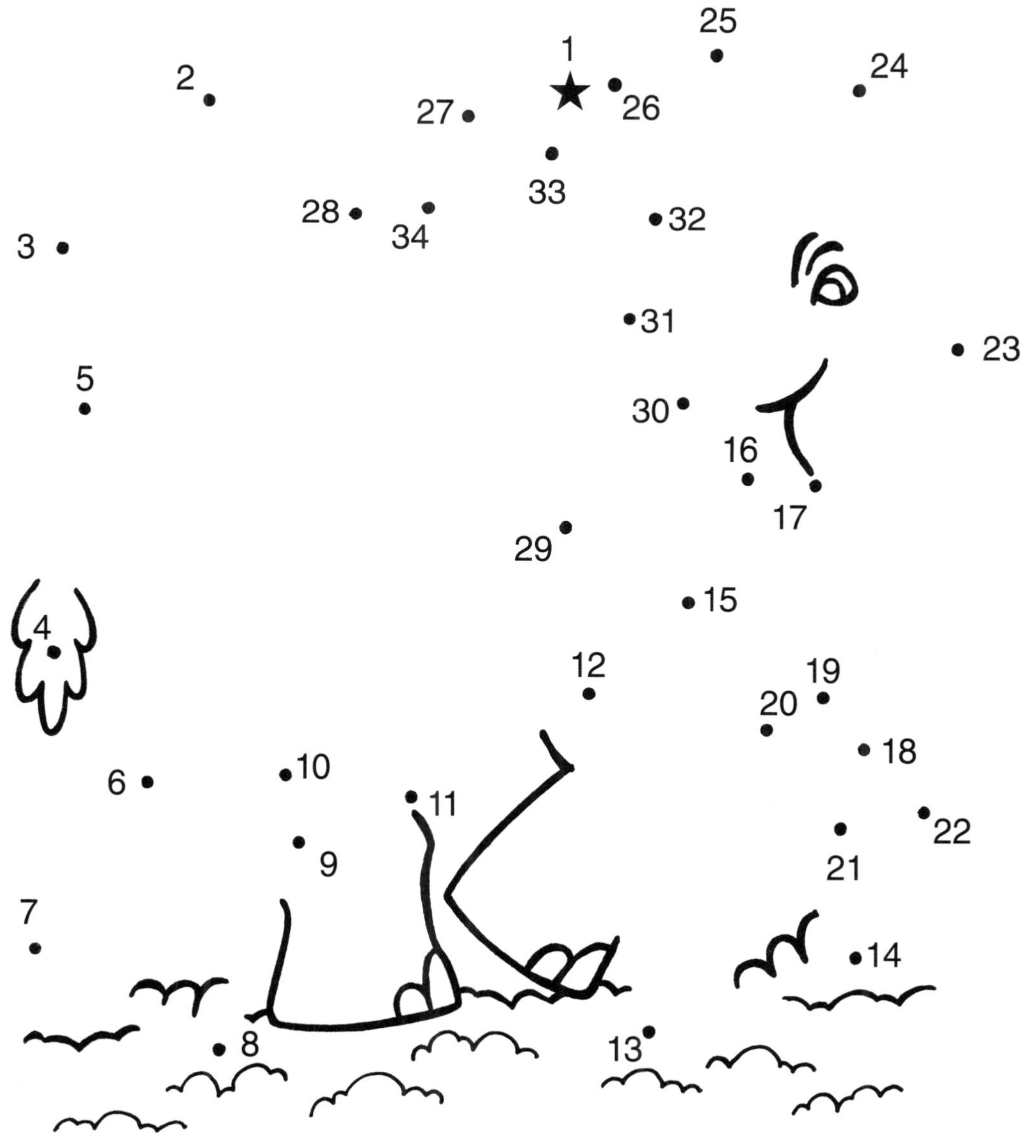

Rhinoceros

Directions: Connect the dots from 1 to 35 to complete the picture.

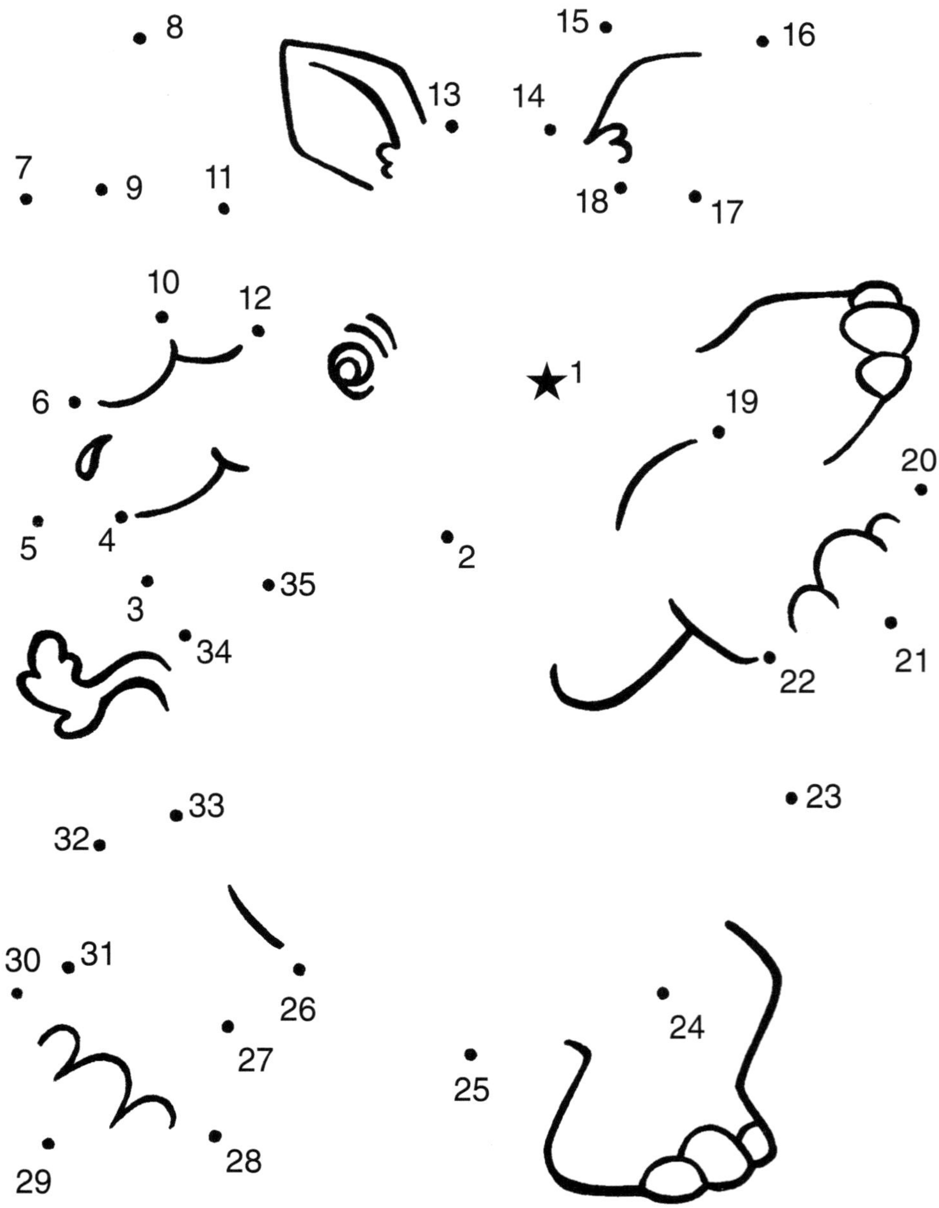

Scarecrow

Directions: Connect the dots from 1 to 35 to complete the picture.

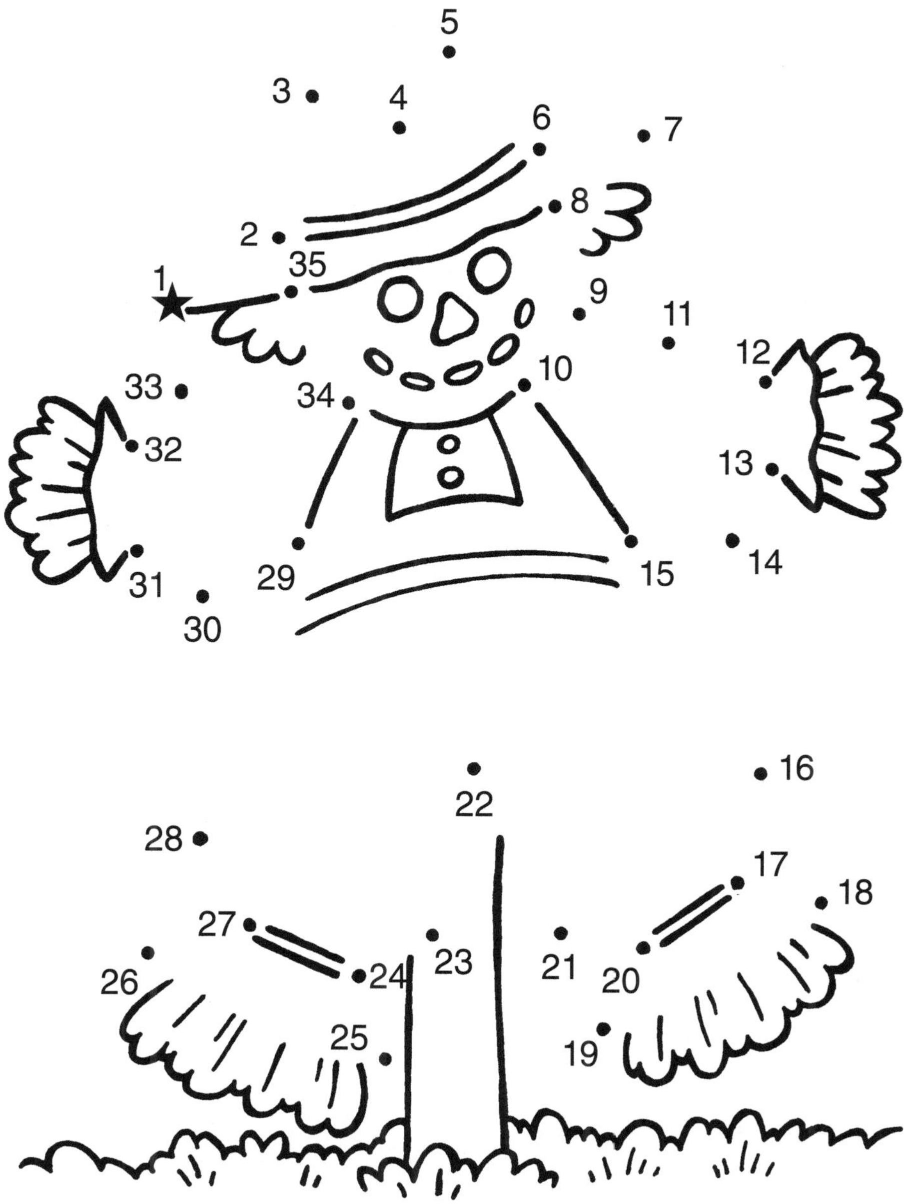

Helicopter

Directions: Connect the dots from 1 to 36 to complete the picture.

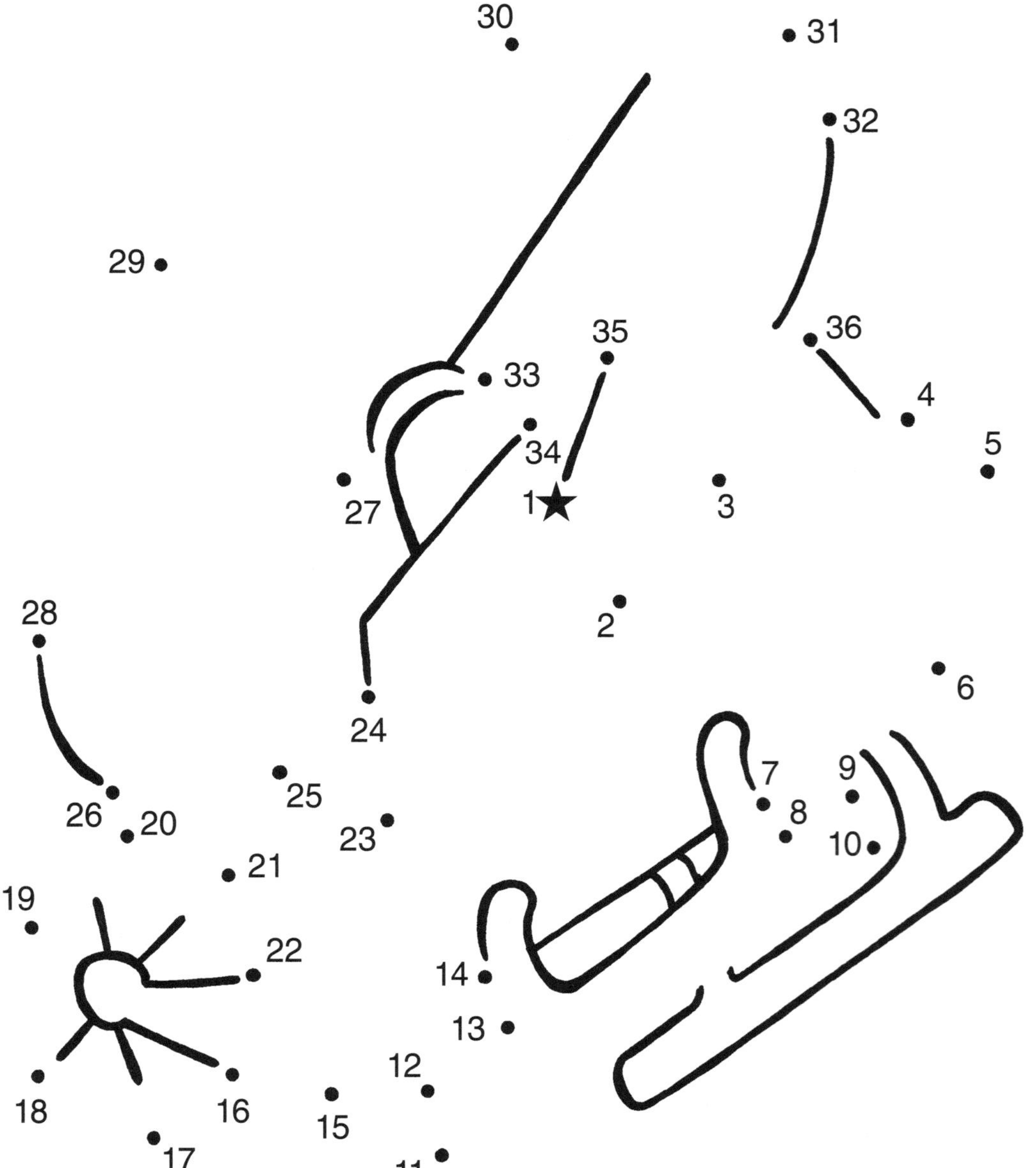

Dive Deep

Directions: Connect the dots from 1 to 37 to complete the picture.

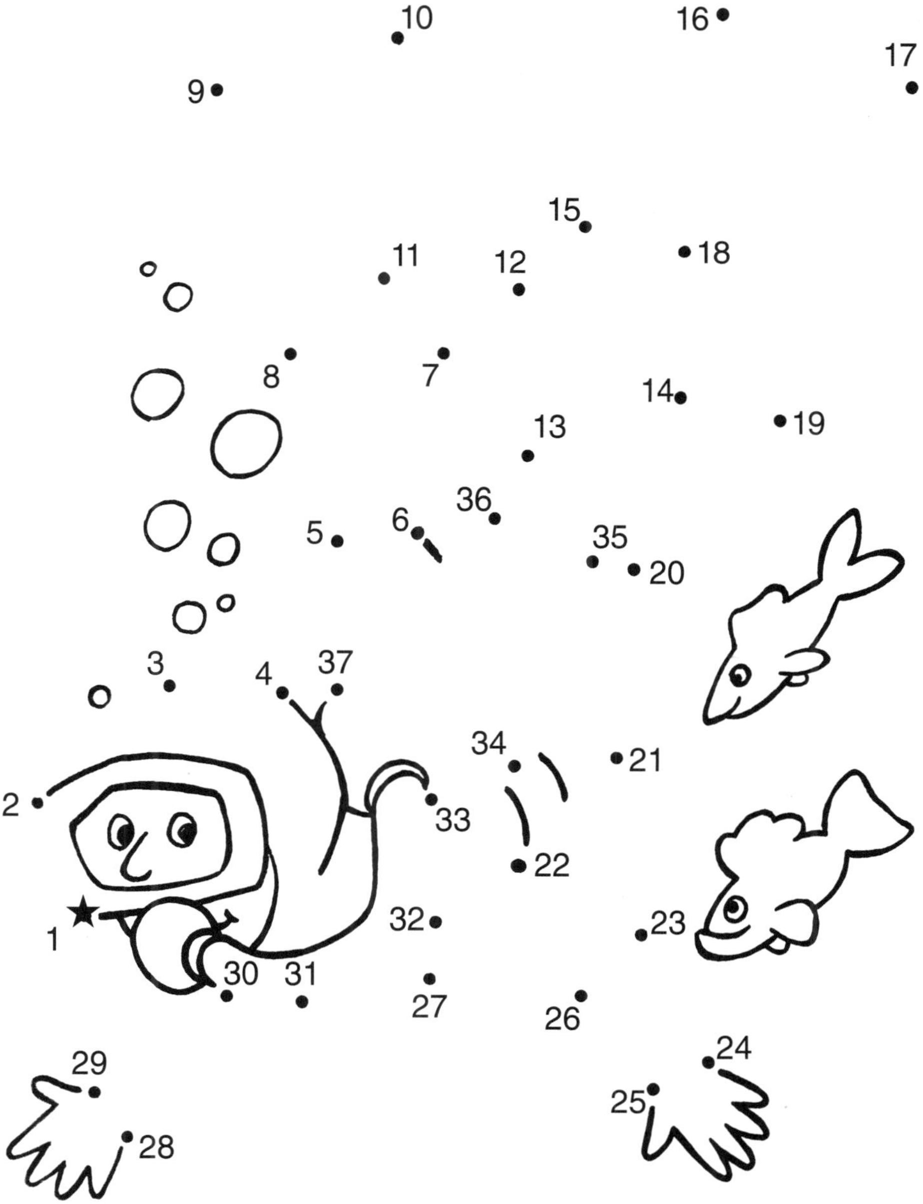

Rocking Horse

Directions: Connect the dots from 1 to 38 to complete the picture.

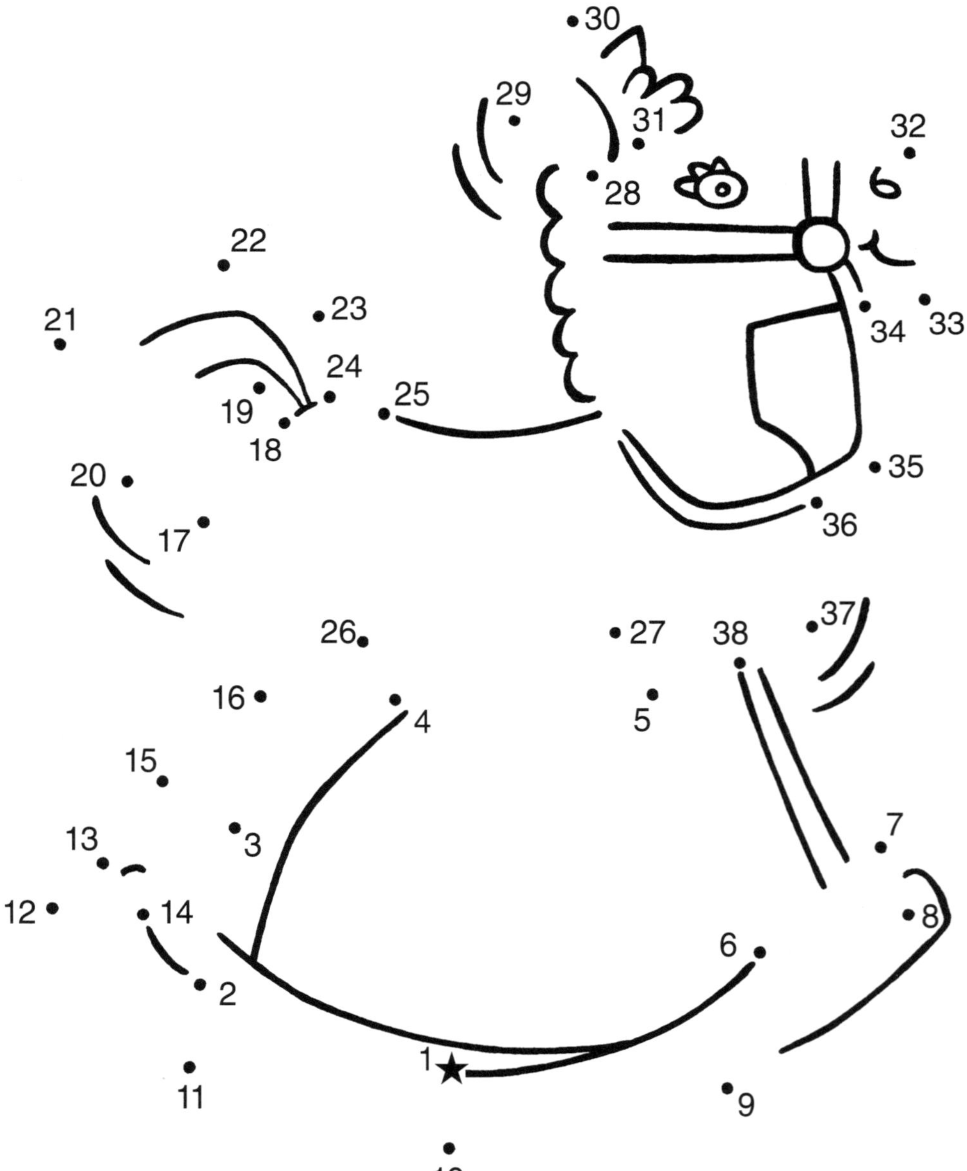

Treasure!

Directions: Connect the dots from 1 to 39 to complete the picture.

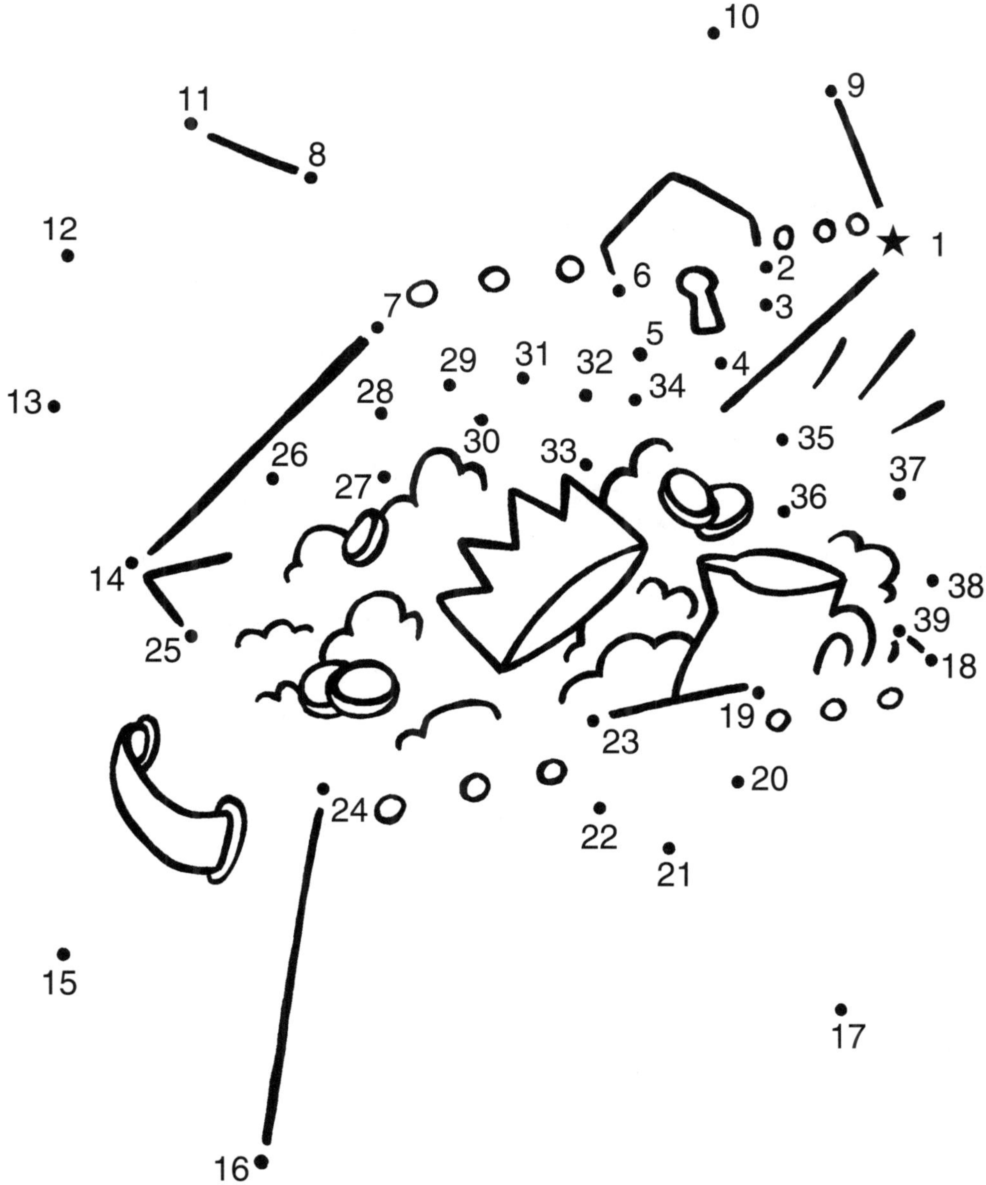

Artist

Directions: Connect the dots from 1 to 40 to complete the picture.

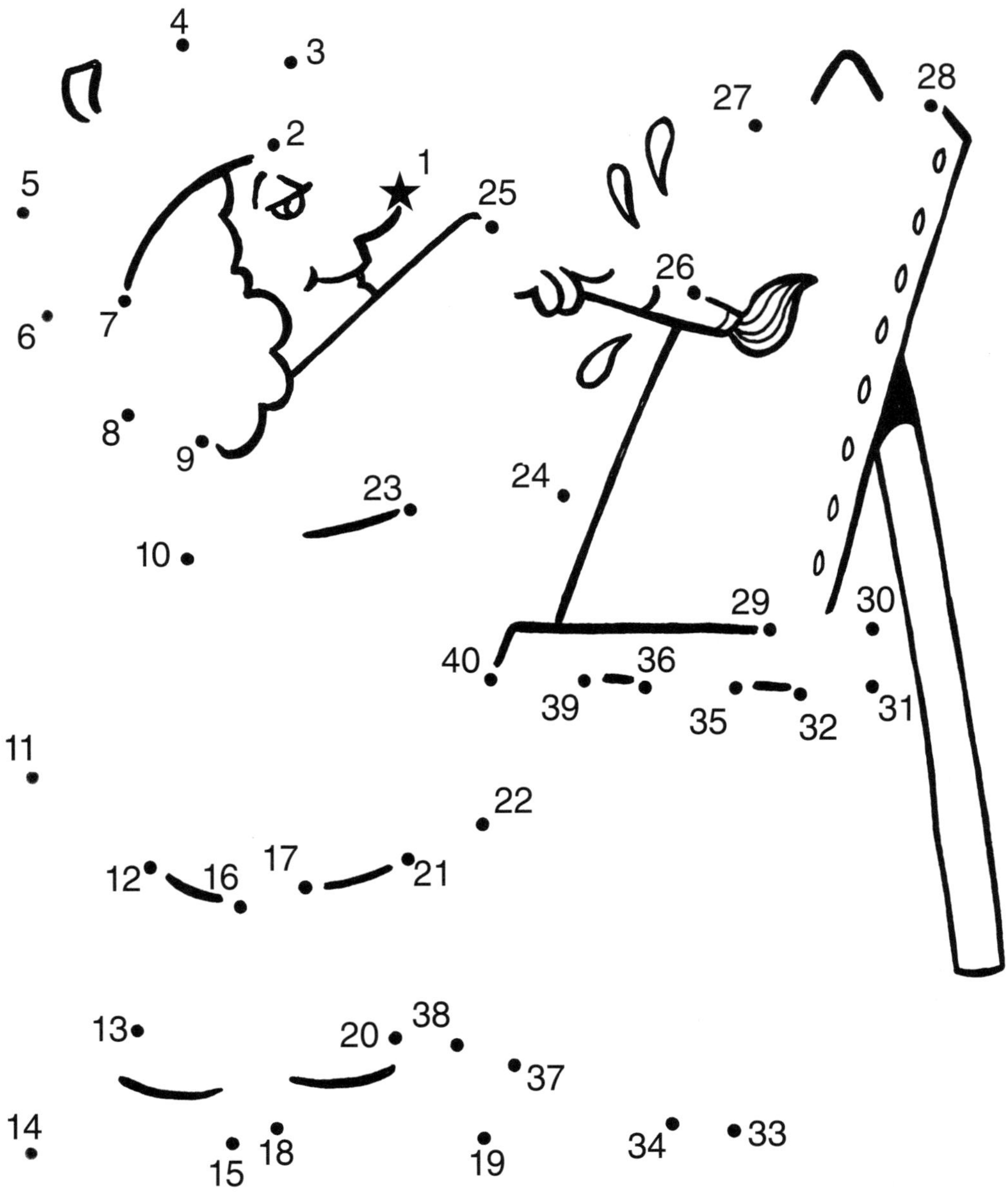

Up and Down

Directions: Connect the dots from 1 to 40 to complete the picture.

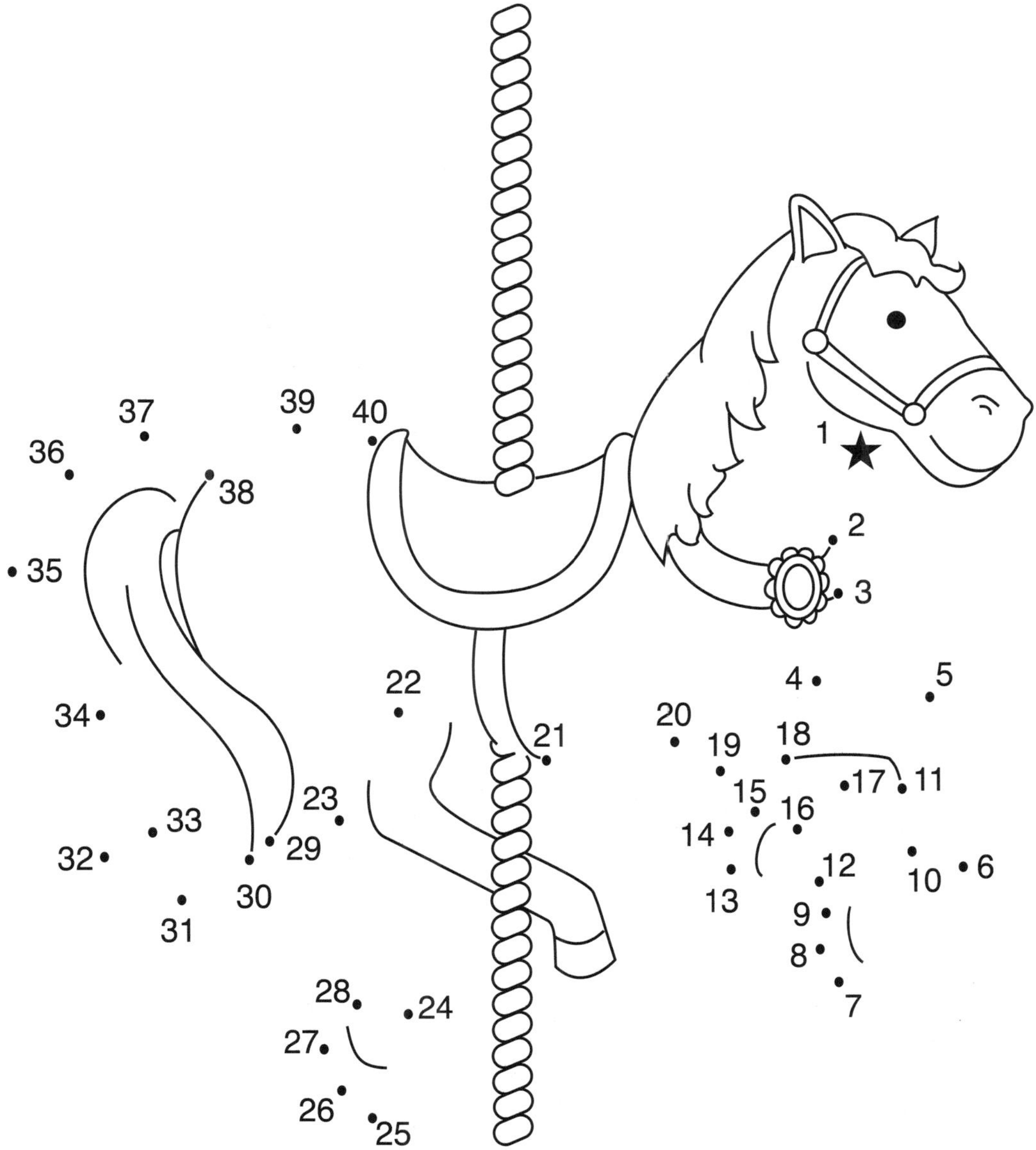

Deer

Directions: Connect the dots from 1 to 40 to complete the picture.

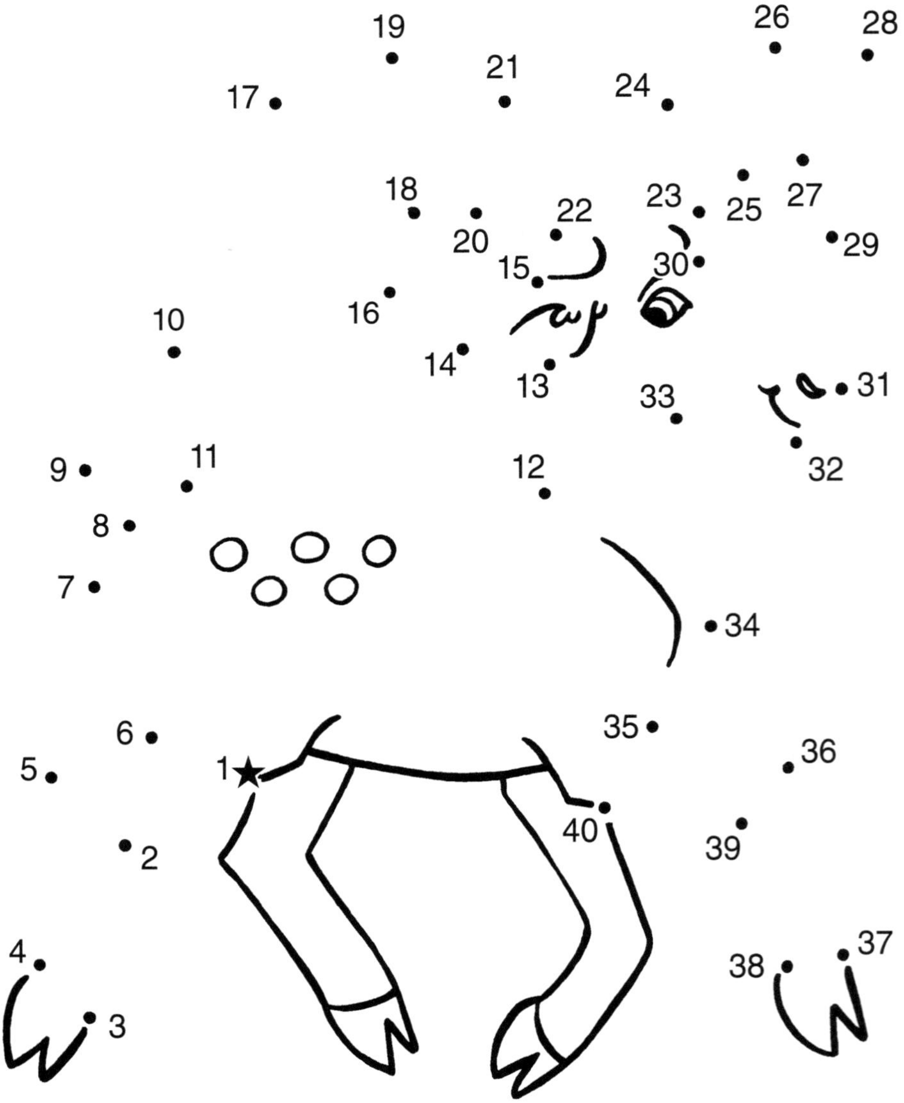

Airplane

Directions: Connect the dots from 1 to 41 to complete the picture.

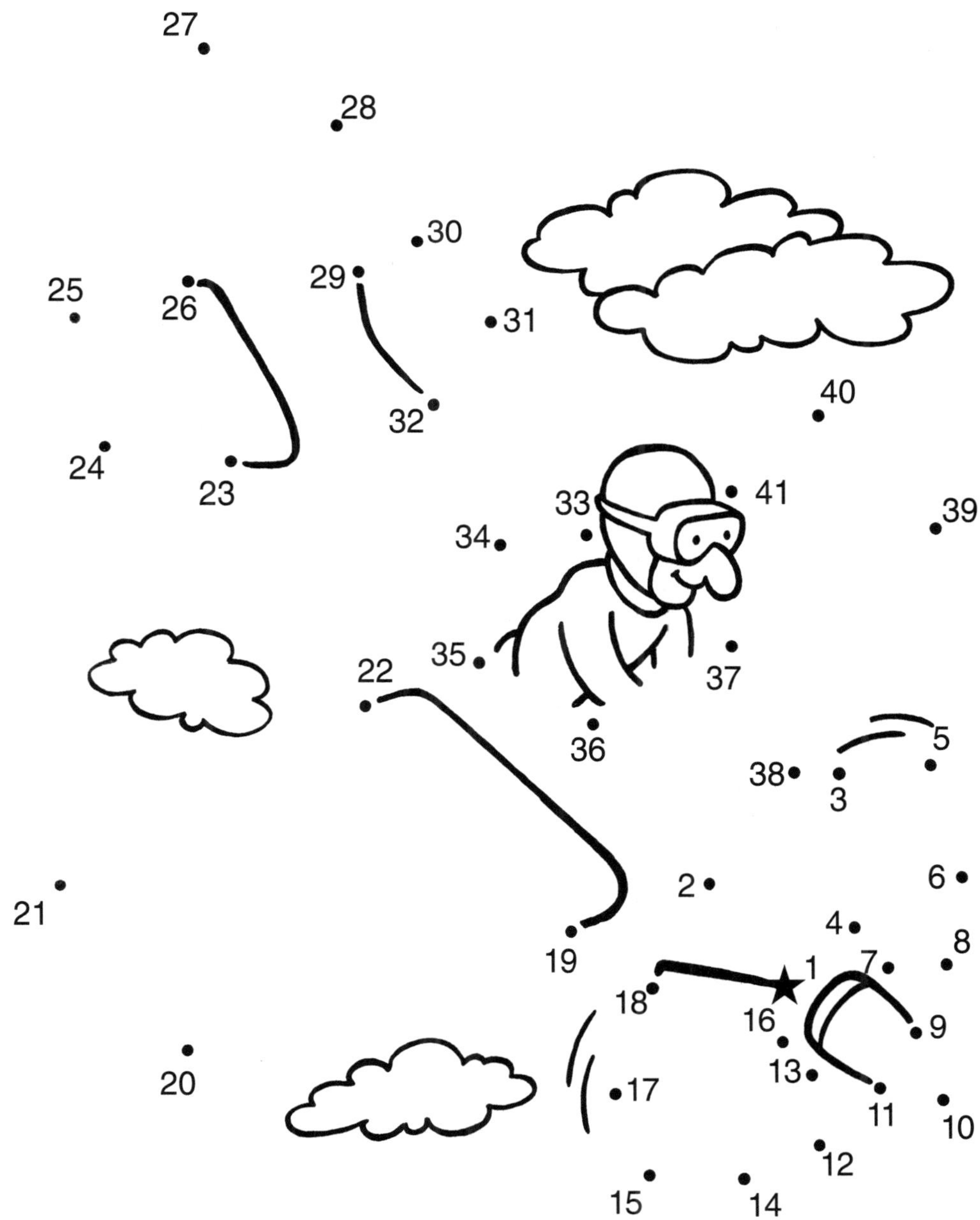

Cow

Directions: Connect the dots from 1 to 42 to complete the picture.

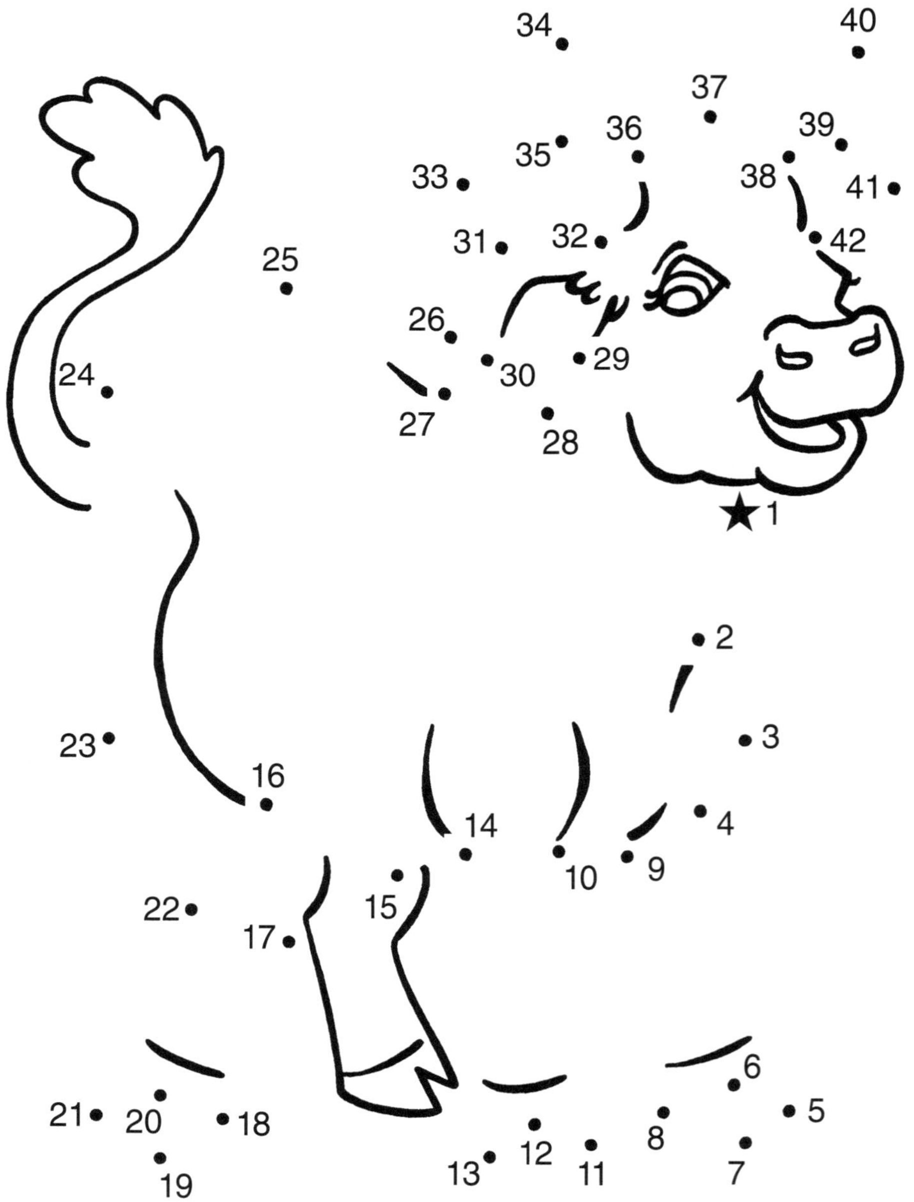

T-Rex

Directions: Connect the dots from 1 to 42 to complete the picture.

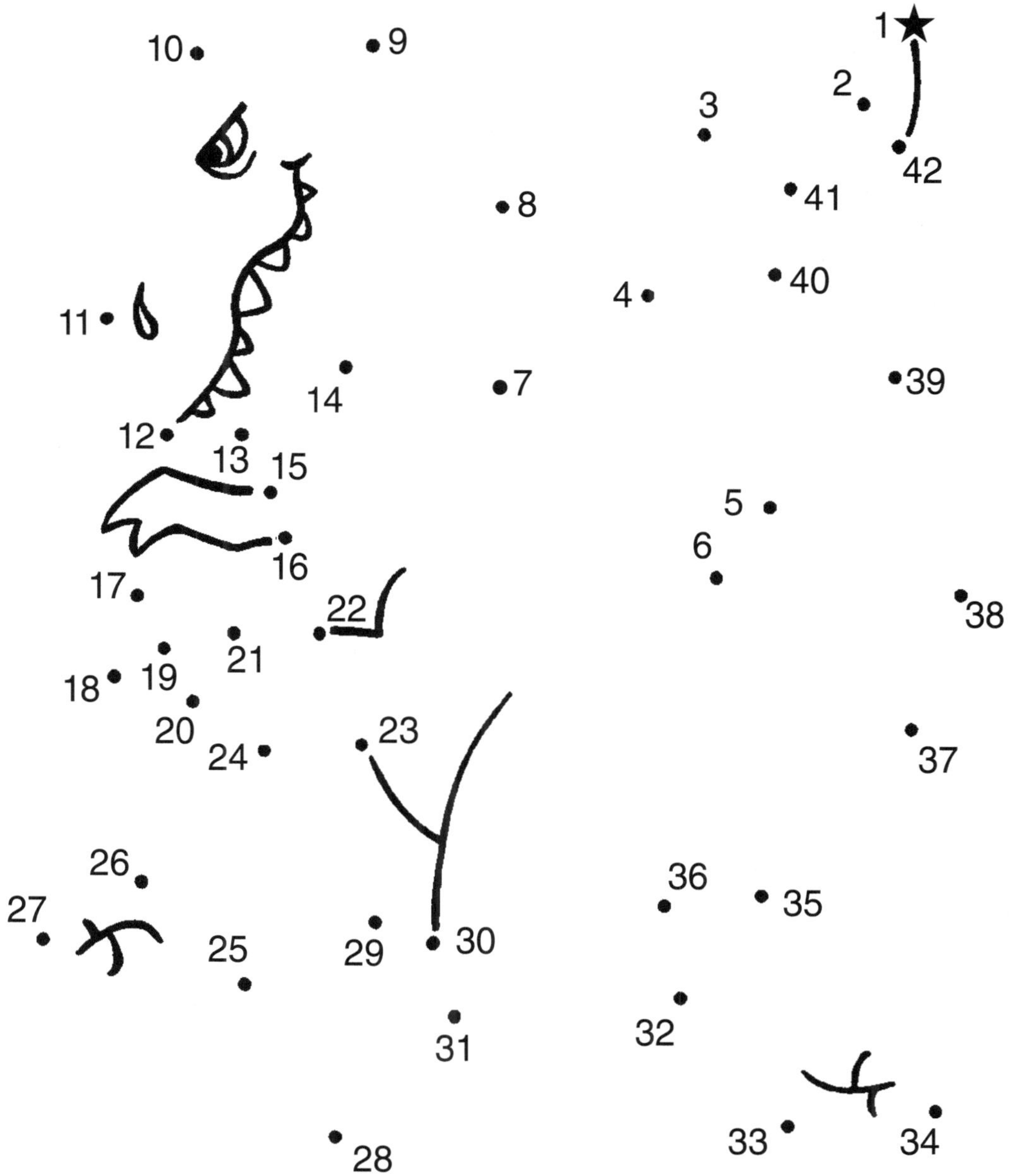

Oink, Oink!

Directions: Connect the dots from 1 to 43 to complete the picture.

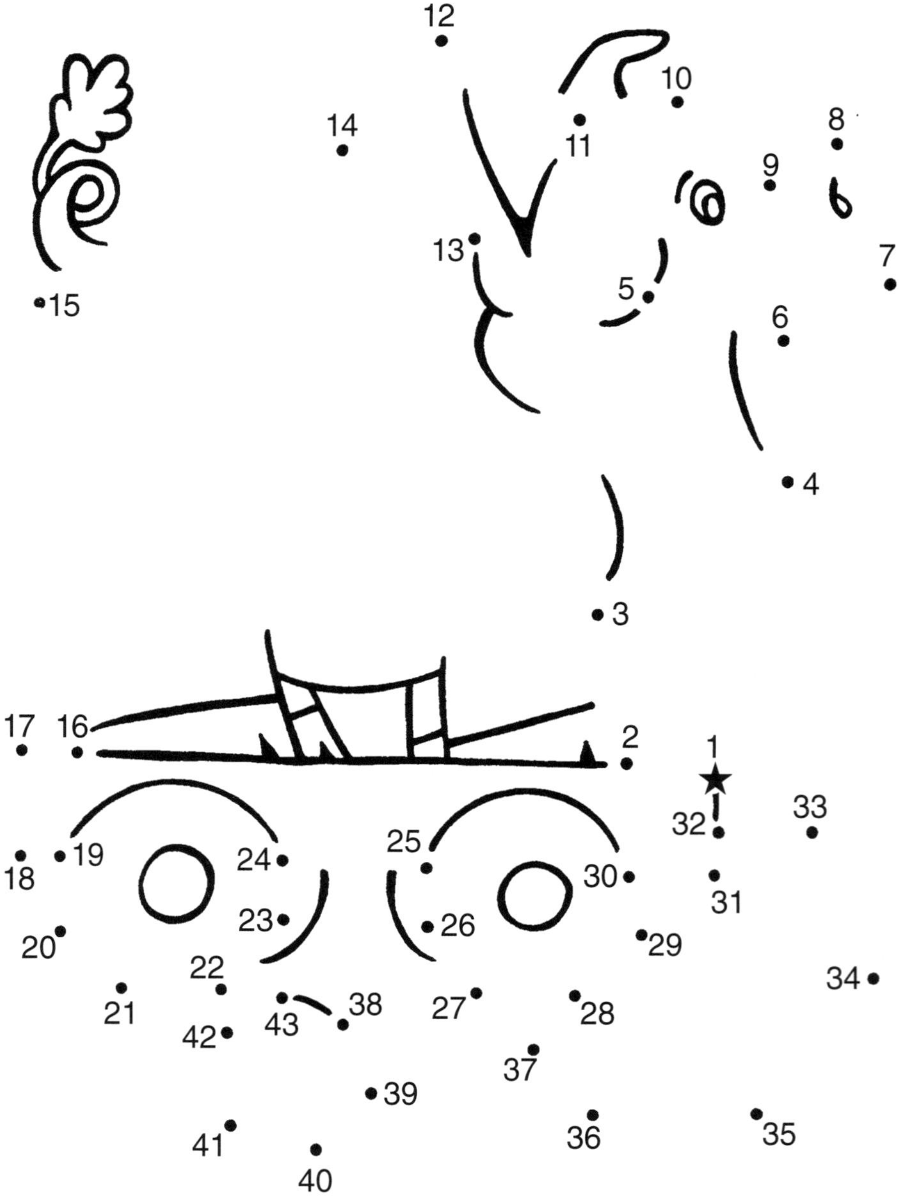

Summer Fun

Directions: Connect the dots from 1 to 44 to complete the picture.

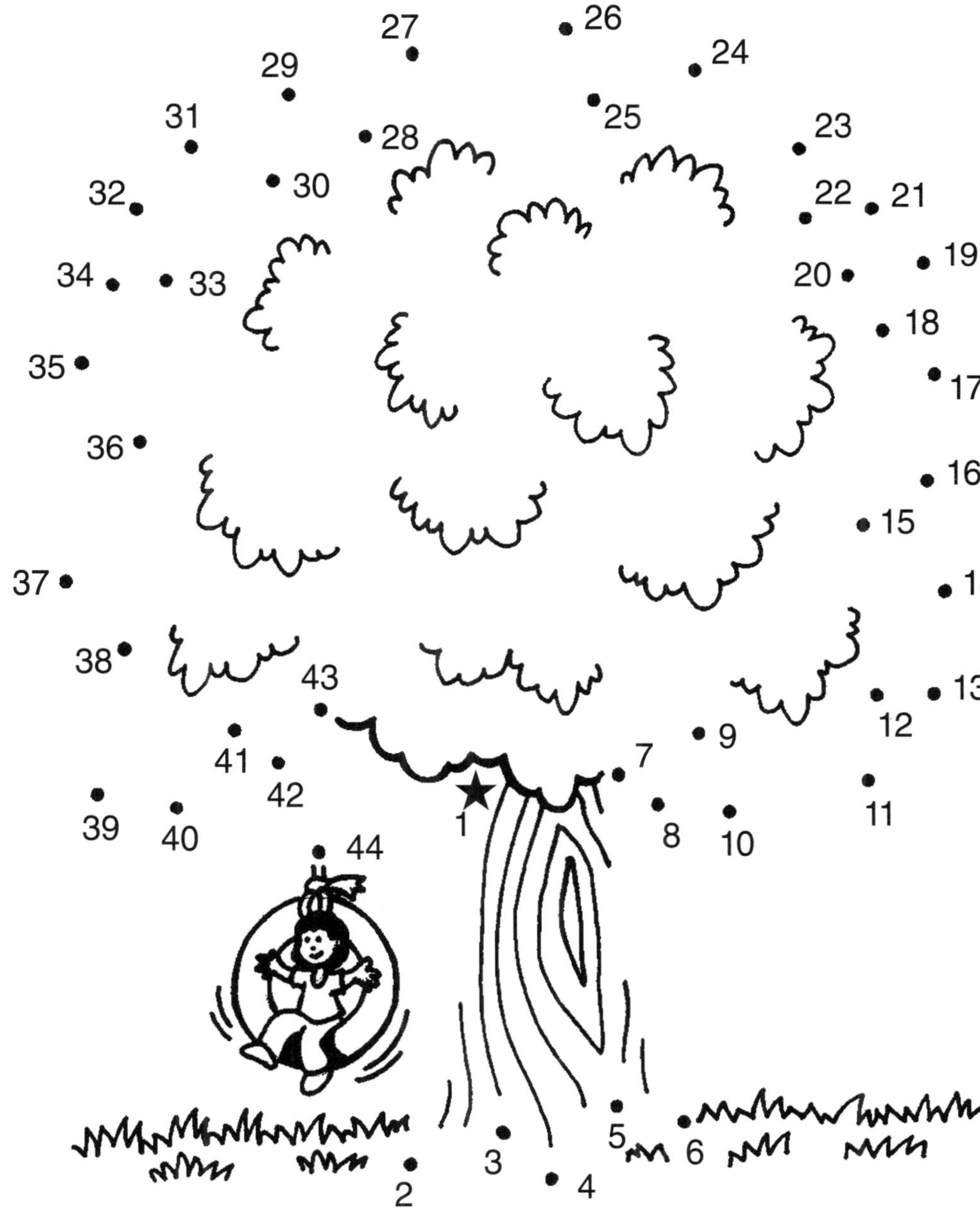

Lizard

Directions: Connect the dots from 1 to 45 to complete the picture.

Digging Up Dirt

Directions: Connect the dots from 1 to 45 to complete the picture.

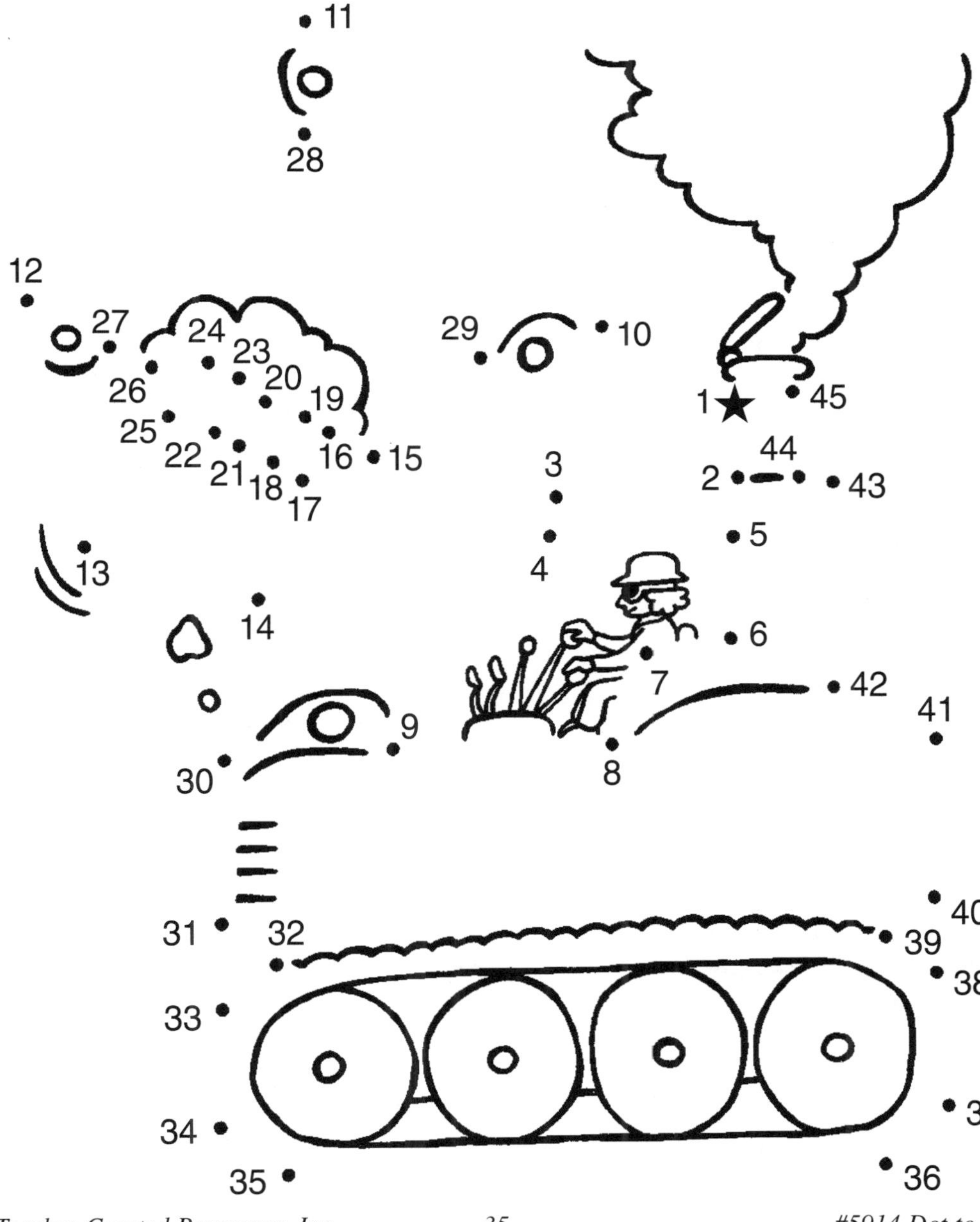

Drive Time

Directions: Connect the dots from 1 to 46 to complete the picture.

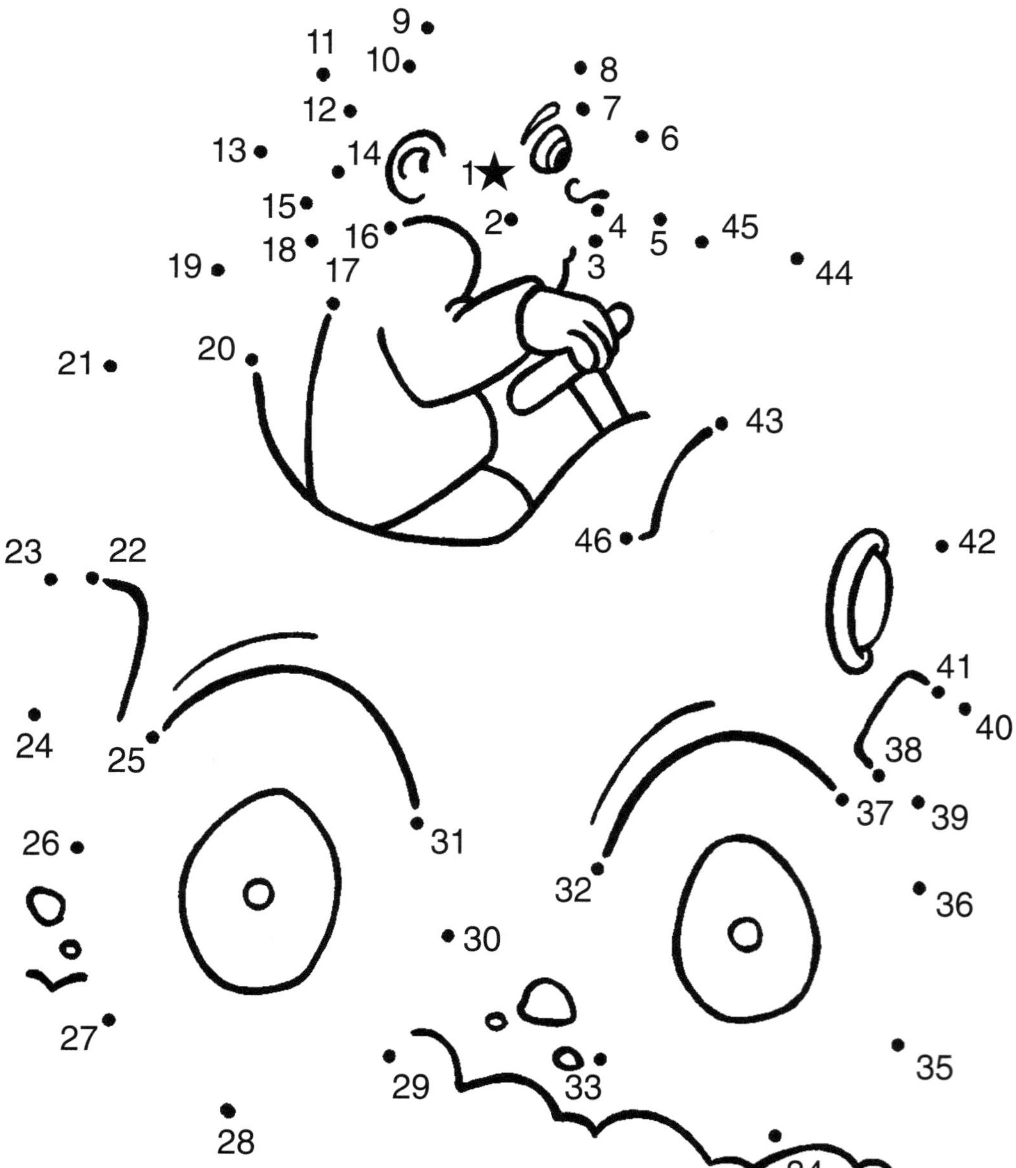

Goat

Directions: Connect the dots from 1 to 47 to complete the picture.

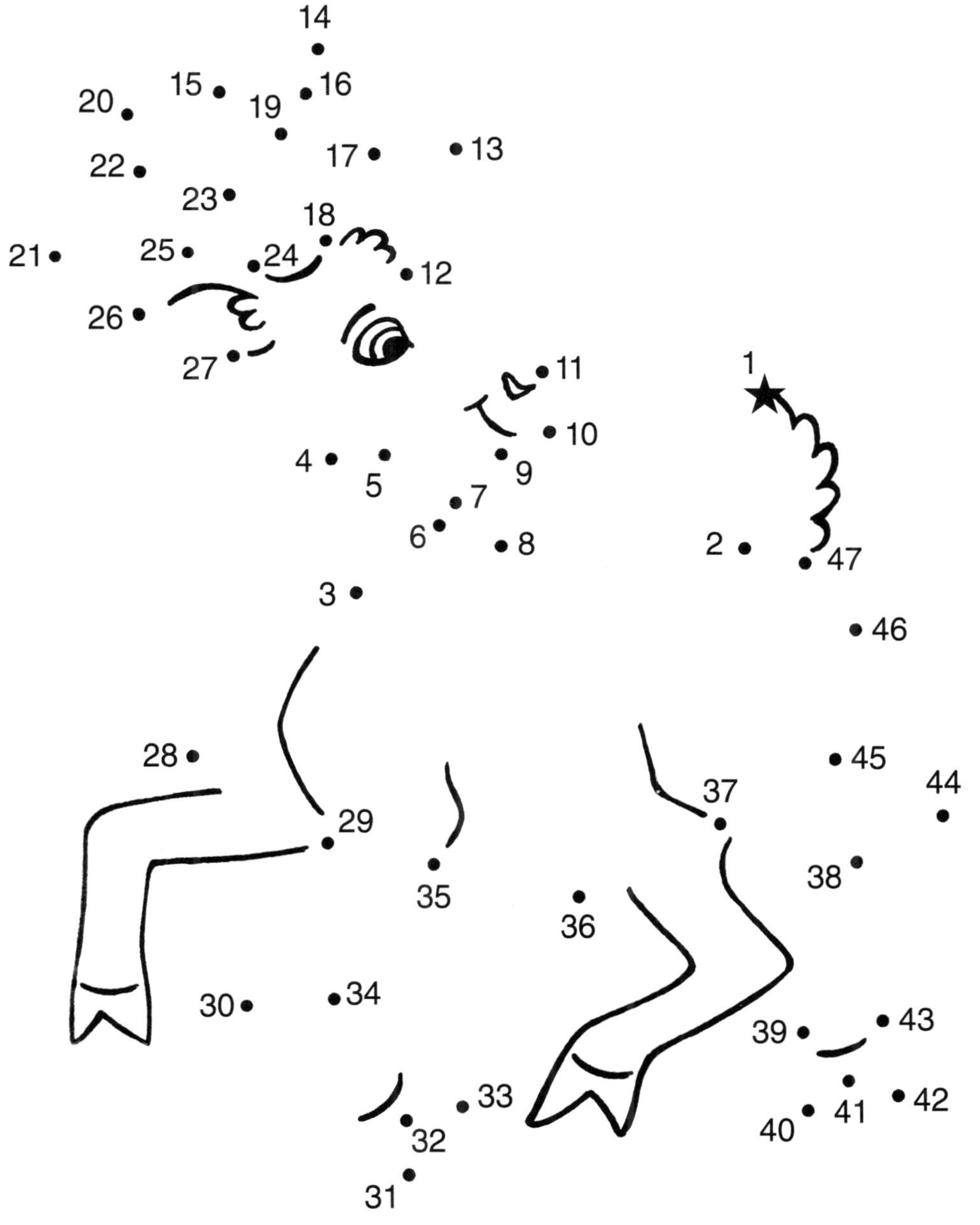

Tiger

Directions: Connect the dots from 1 to 48 to complete the picture.

Lion

Directions: Connect the dots from 1 to 49 to complete the picture.

How Many Towers?

Directions: Connect the dots from 1 to 50 to complete the picture.

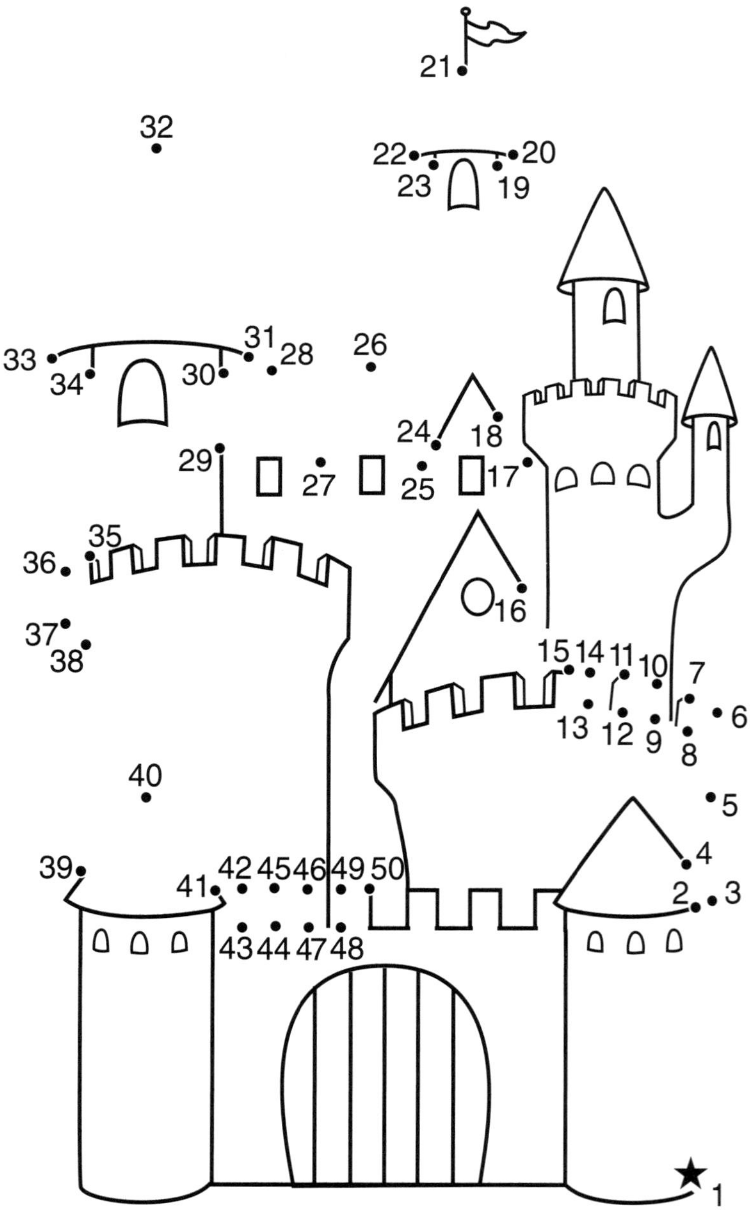

Monkey

Directions: Connect the dots from 1 to 50 to complete the picture.

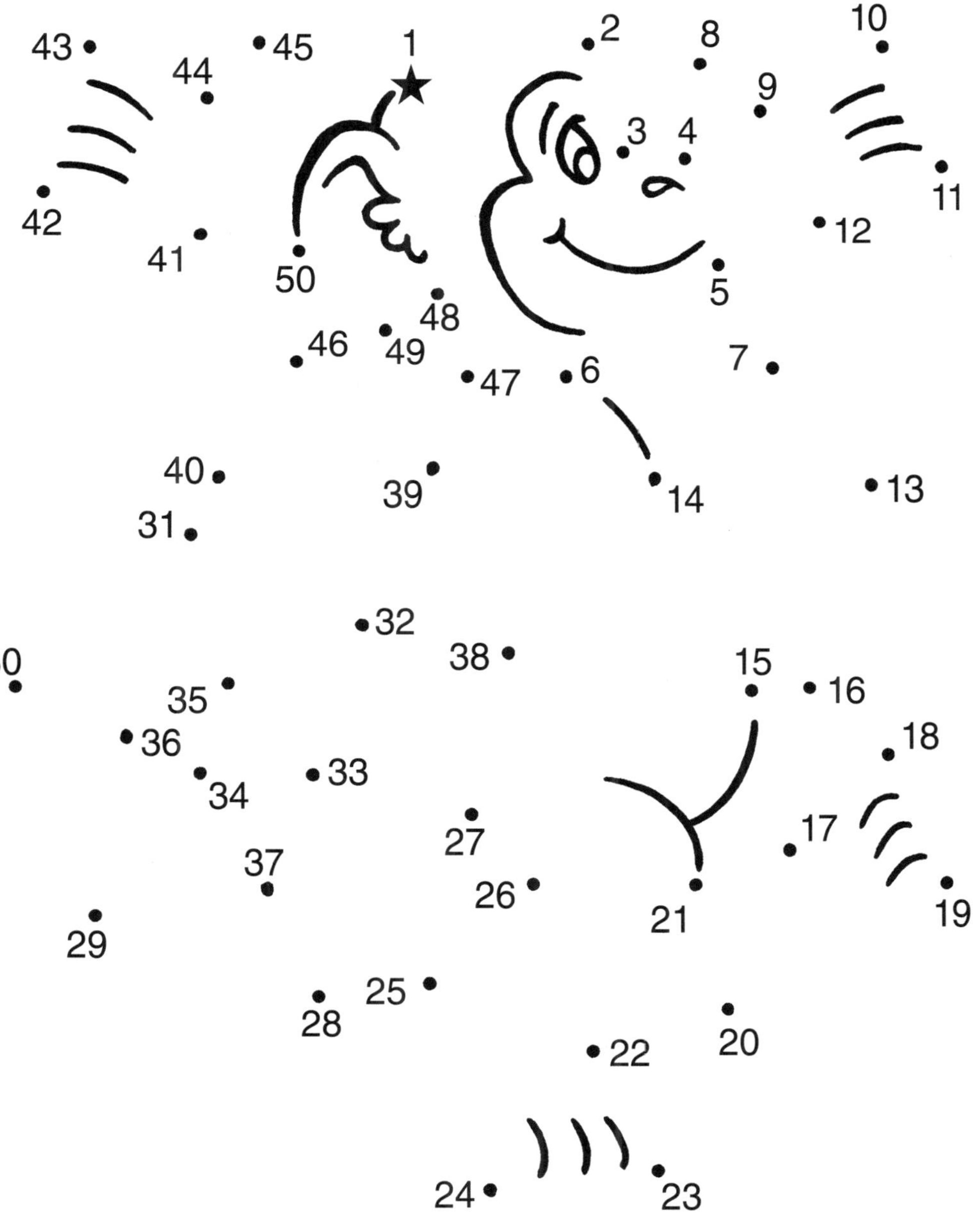

Puppy

Directions: Connect the dots from 1 to 50 to complete the picture.

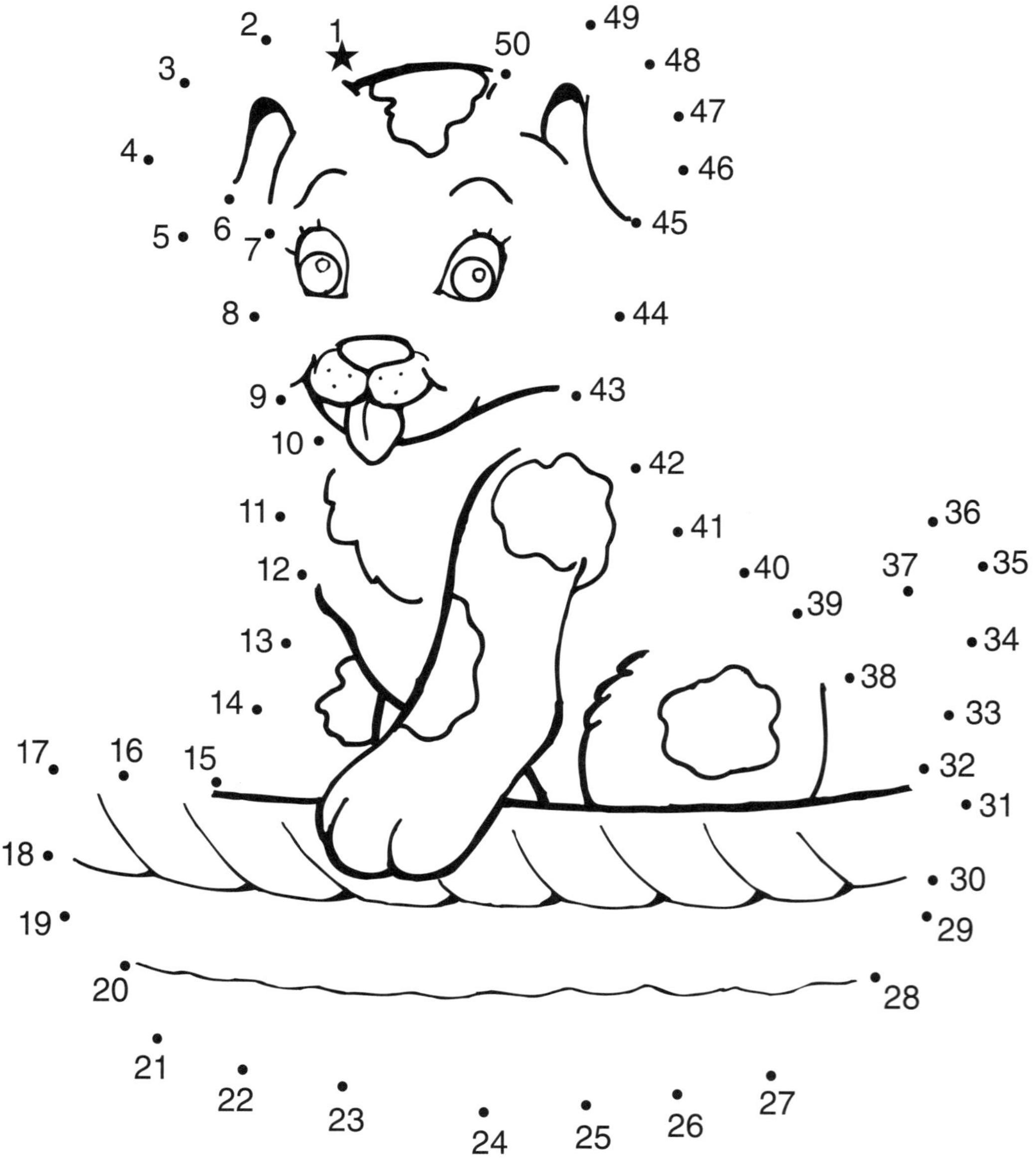

Cheese Time

Directions: Connect the dots from 1 to 50 to complete the picture.

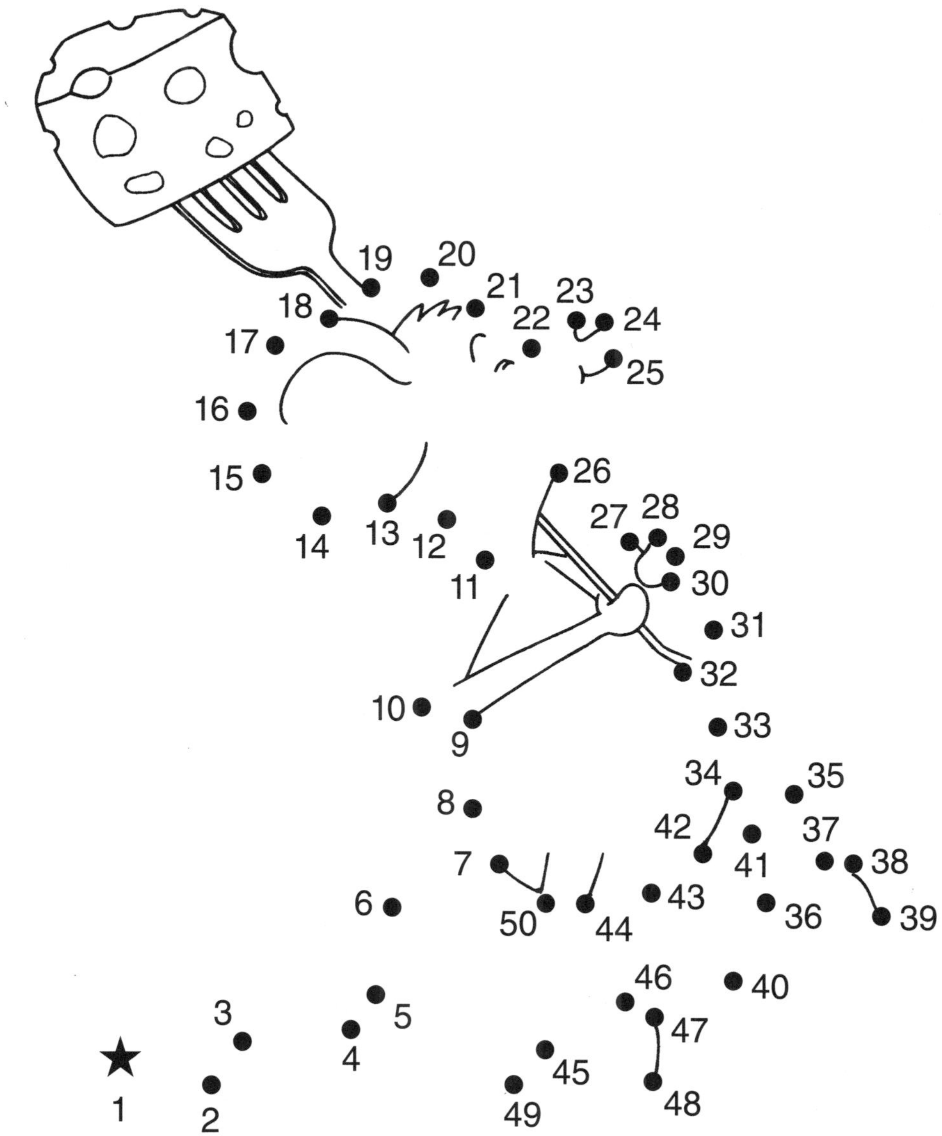

Flowers

Directions: Connect the dots from 1 to 50 to complete the picture.

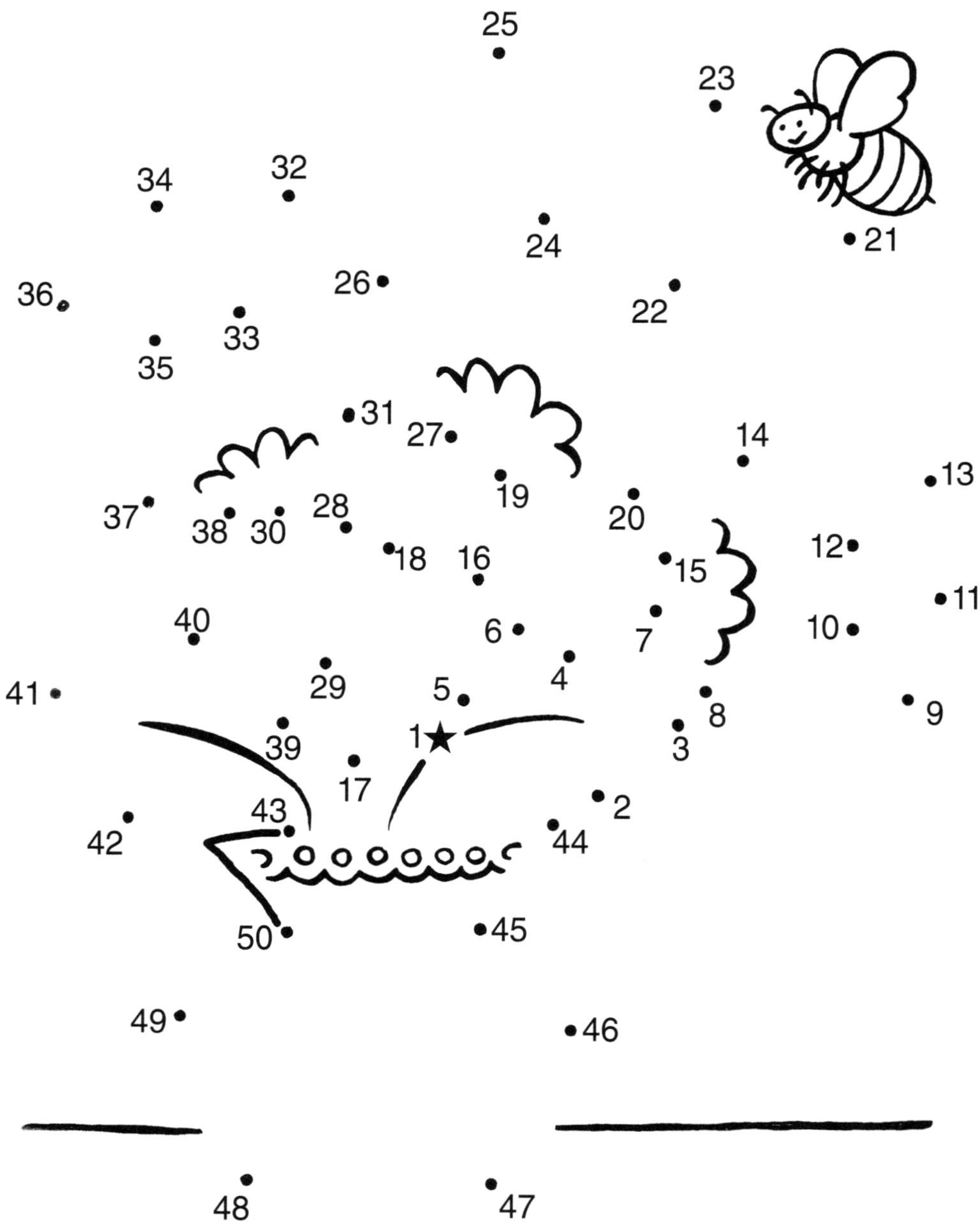

Brave Knight

Directions: Connect the dots from 1 to 60 to complete the picture.

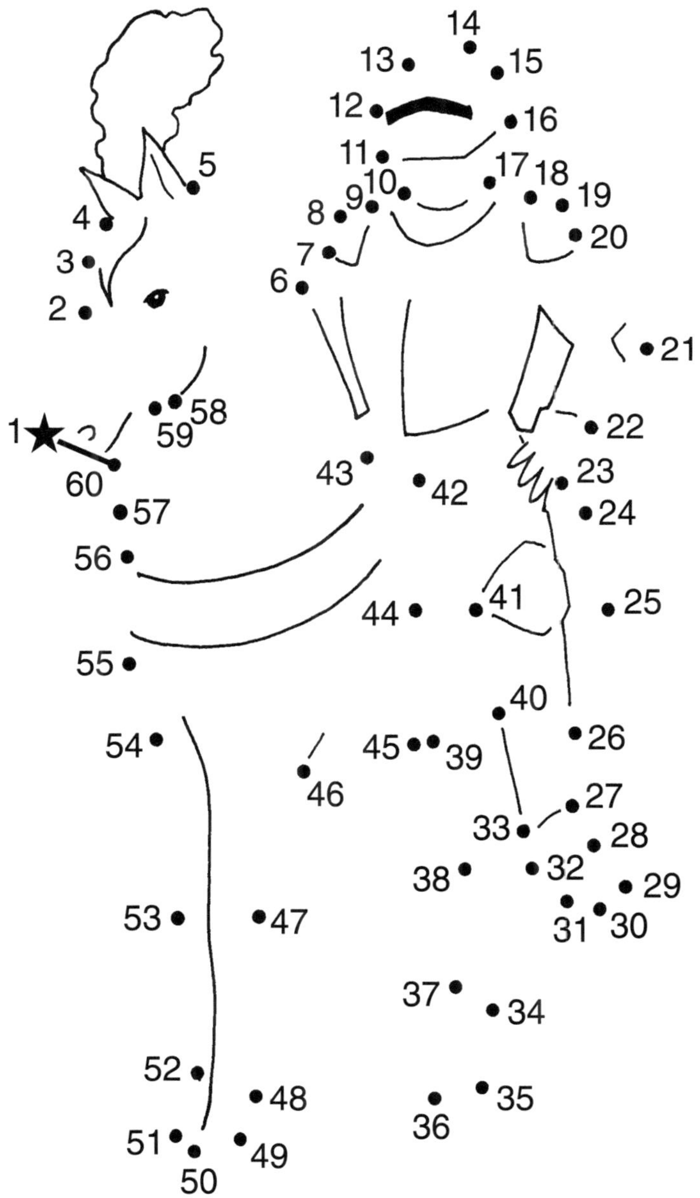

Sensational Snake

Directions: Connect the dots from 1 to 66 to complete the picture.

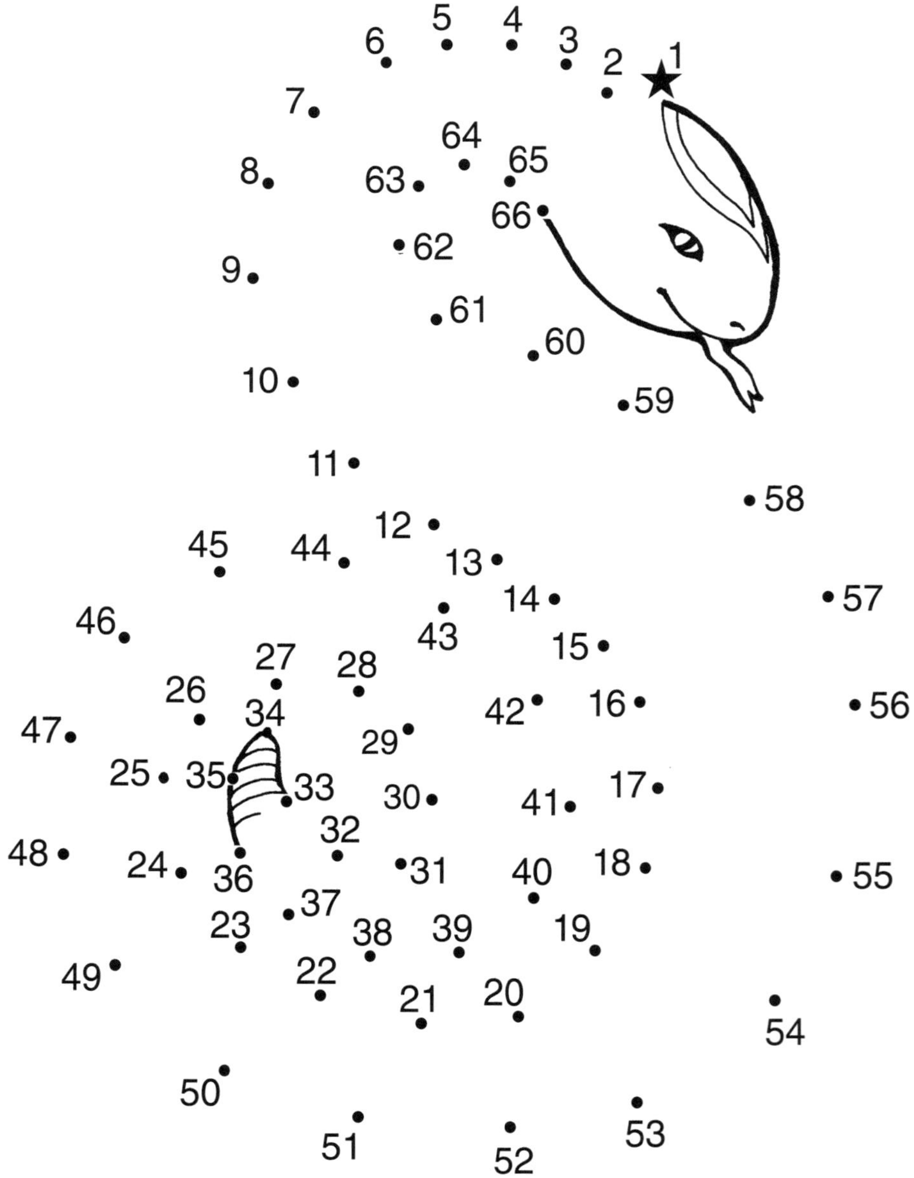

Giraffe

Directions: Connect the dots from 50 to 100 to complete the picture.

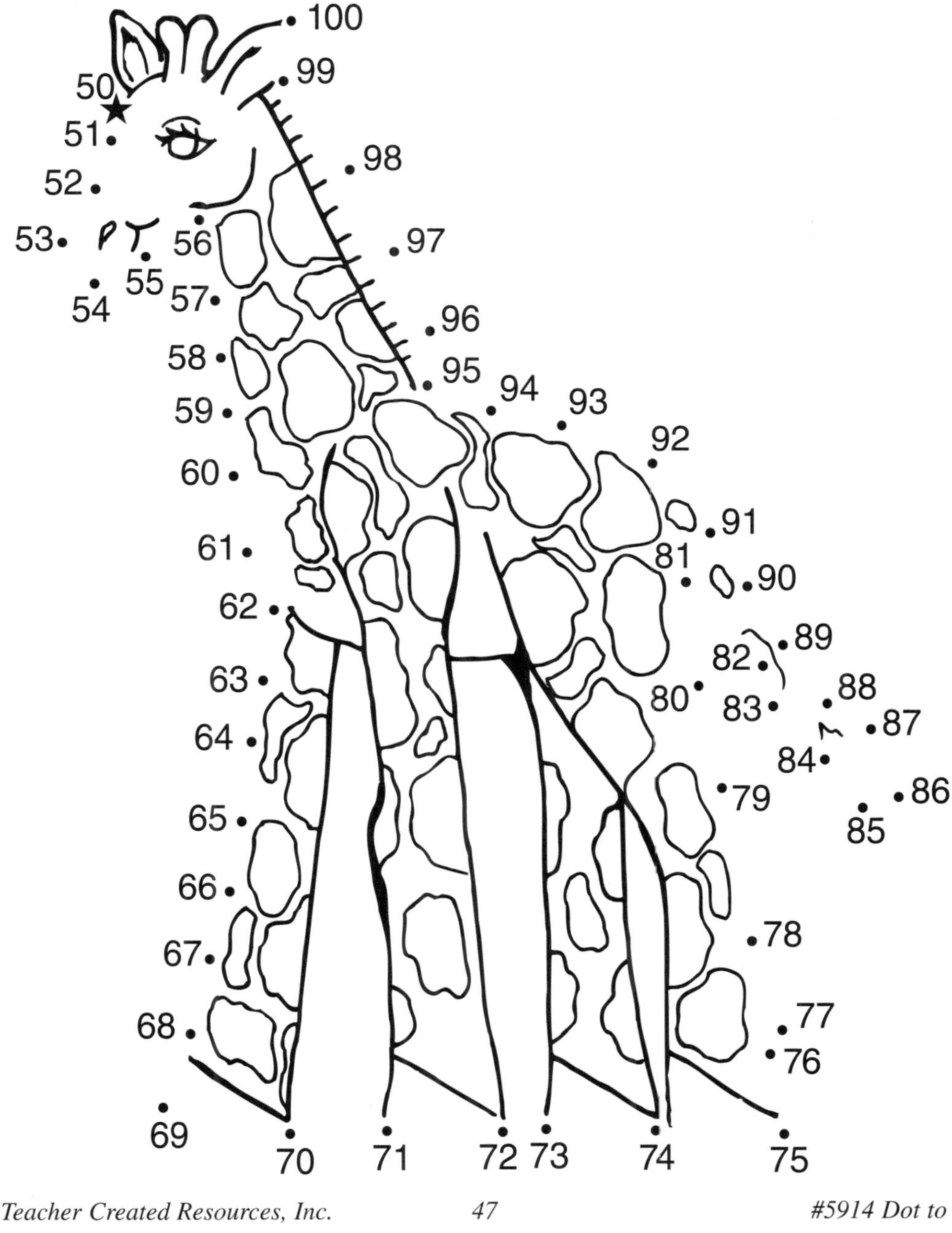

Gingerbread

Directions: Connect the dots from 0 to 100 to complete the picture.

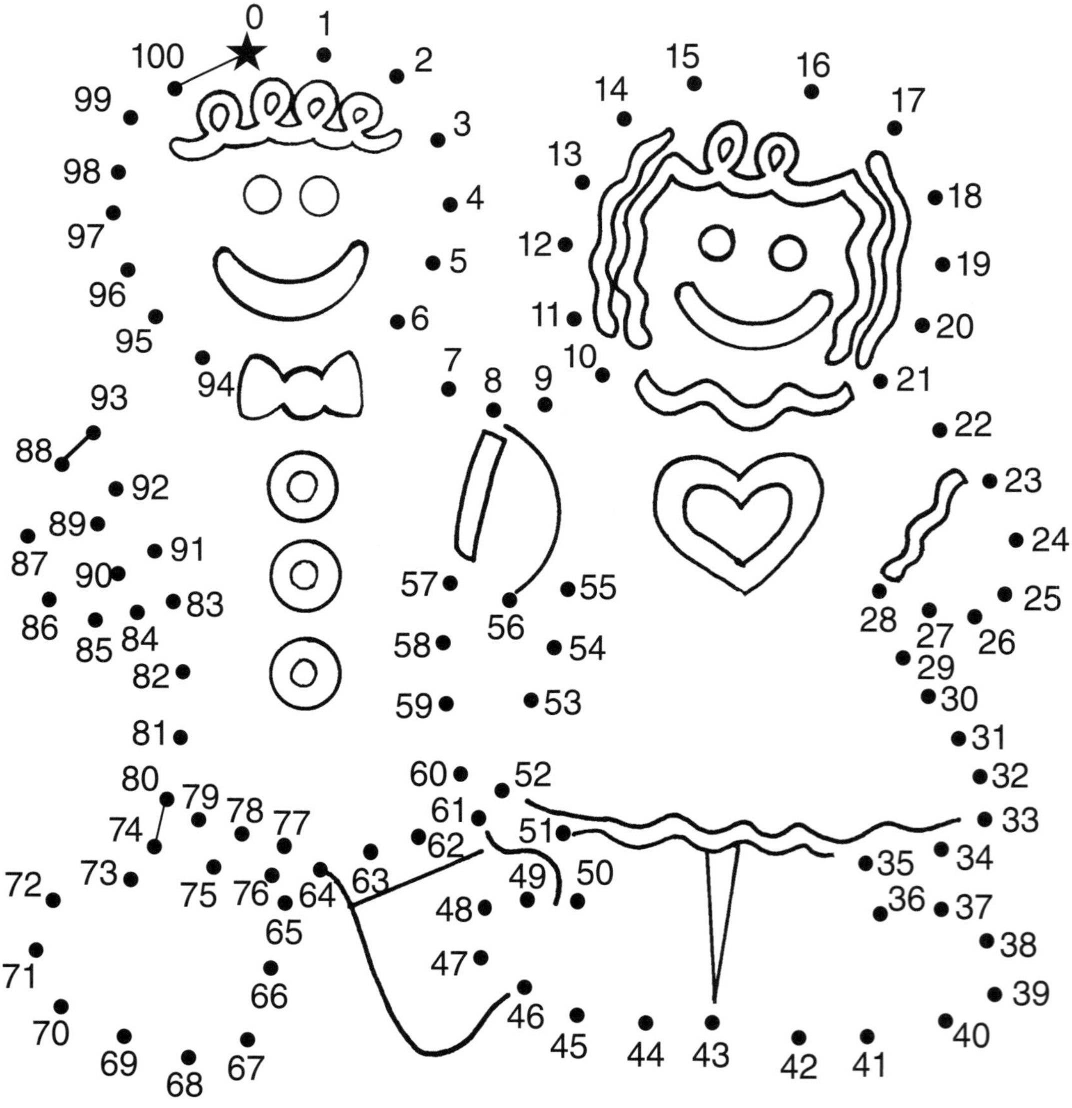

Octopus

Directions: Connect the dots from 1 to 100 to complete the picture.

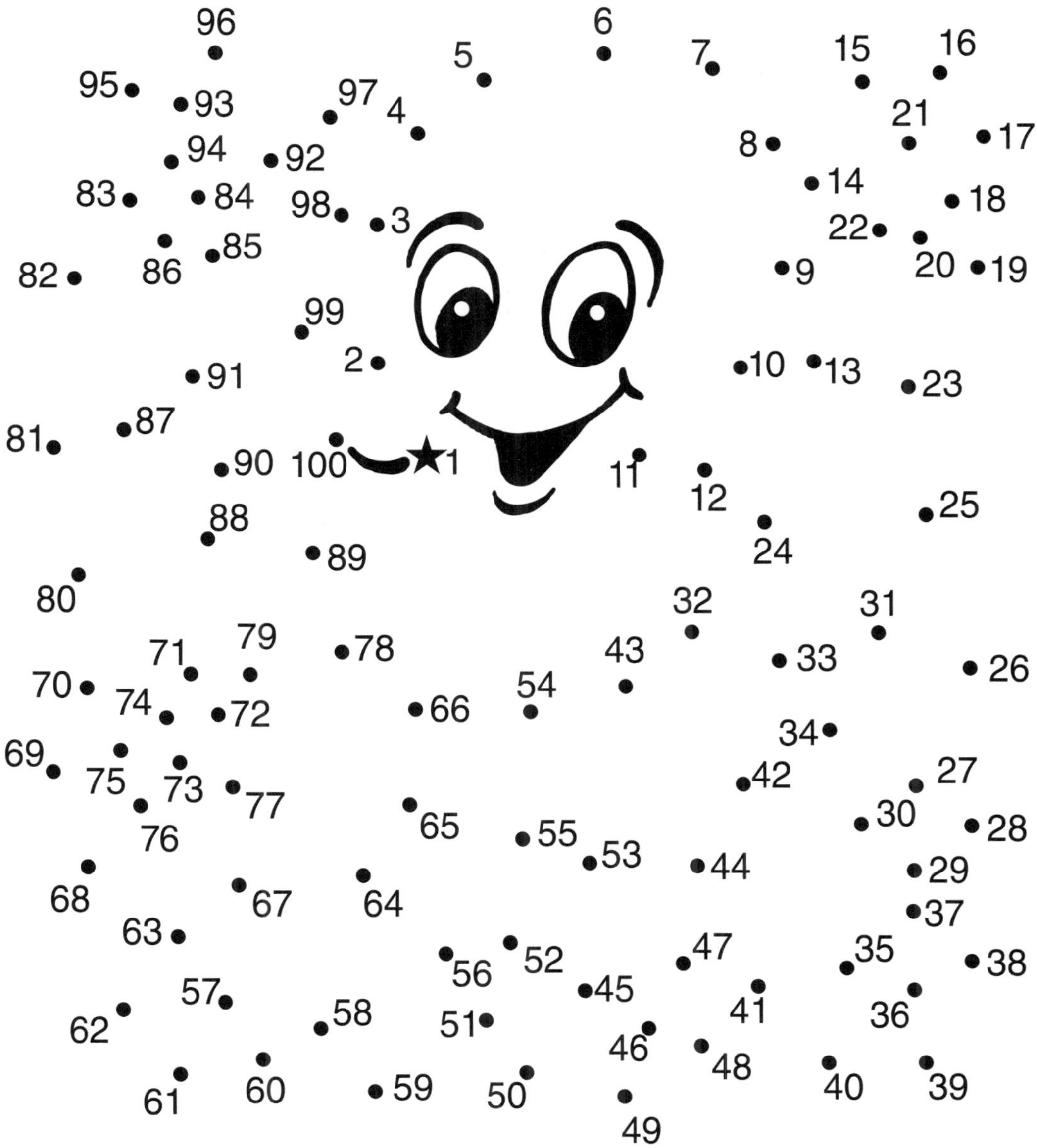

Creating Shapes

Directions: Join the numbers to make shapes. Name the shapes.

a.

Name: ________________

b.

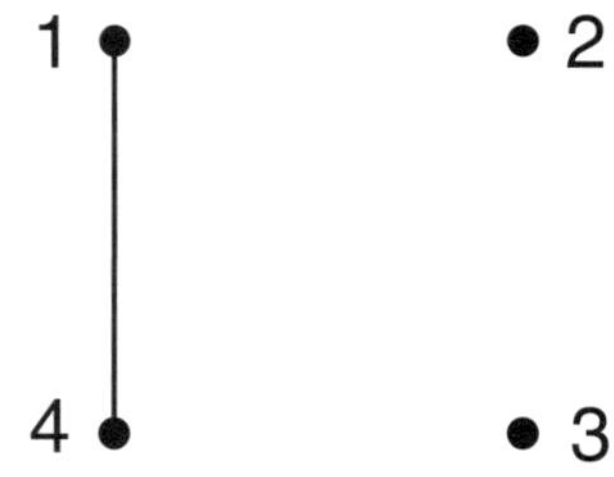

Name: ________________

c.

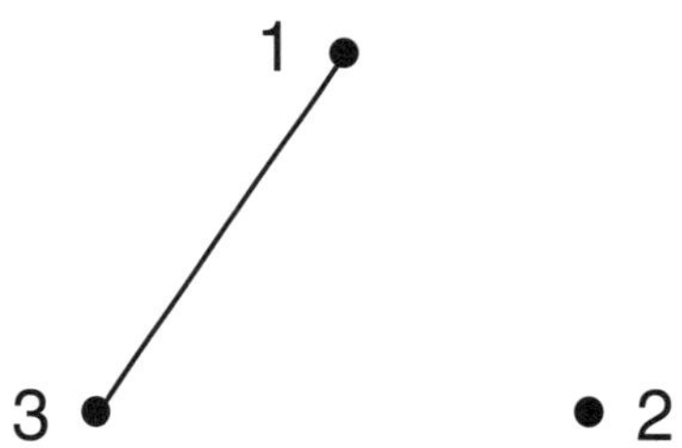

Name: ________________

d.

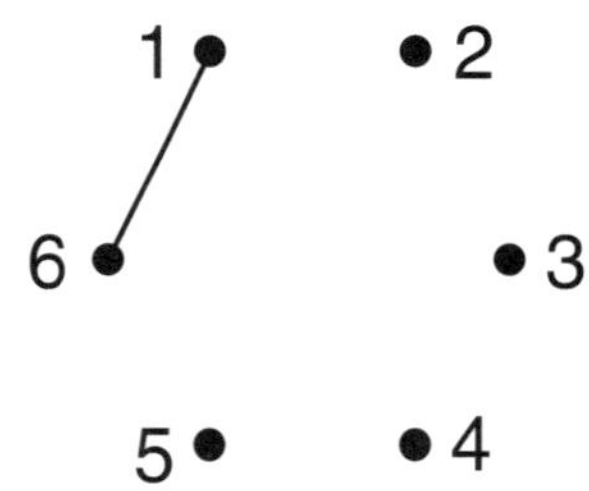

Name: ________________

e.

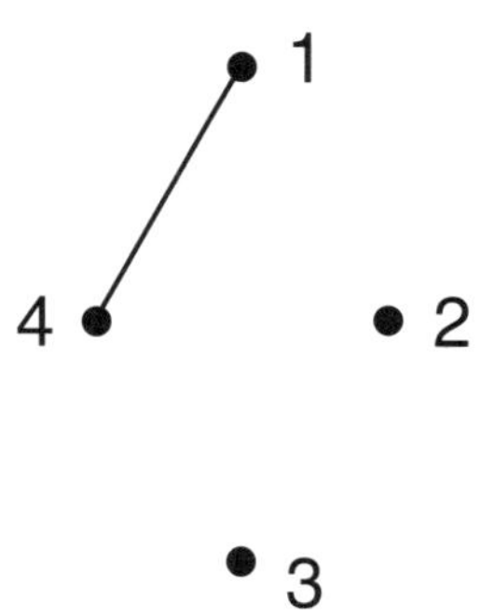

Name: ________________

Joining the Dots by 2s

Directions: Here is a hidden picture. What do you think it might be? Start at 0. Count up by 2s and join the numbers in a line to make the picture. Then join the last number back to 0.

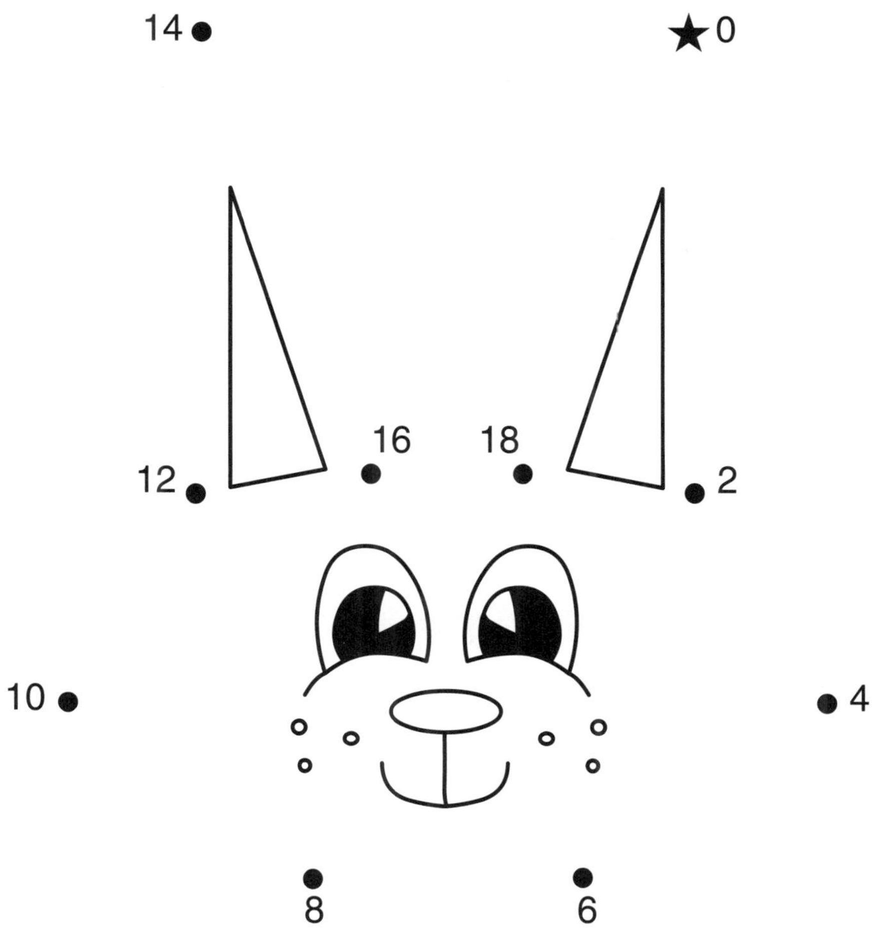

Count by 2s

Directions: Count by 2s and connect the dots to complete the picture.

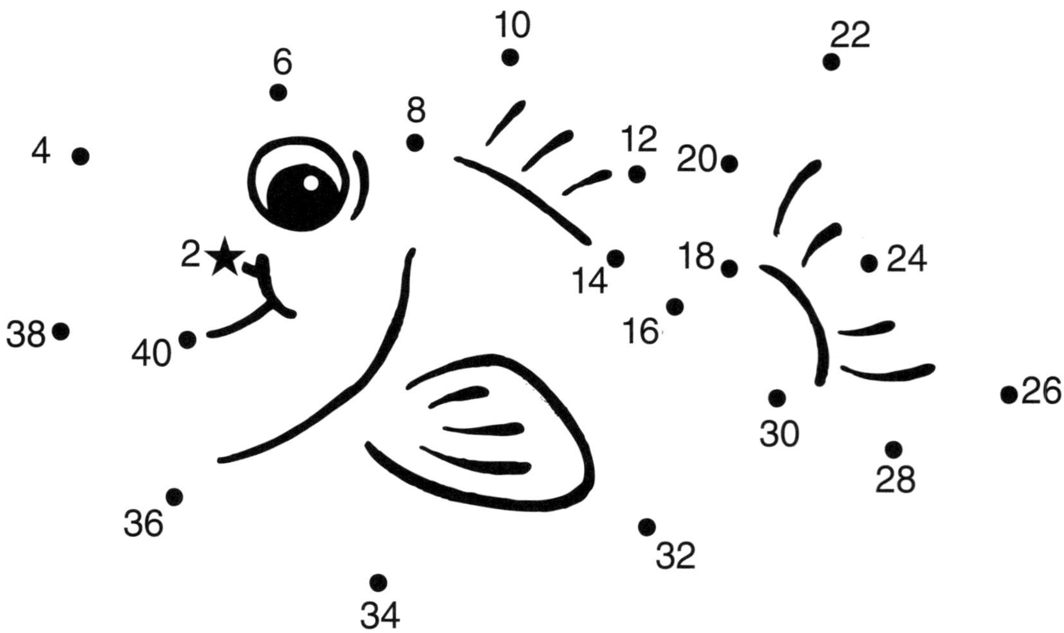

Mountain Home

Directions: Count by 2s and connect the dots to complete the picture.

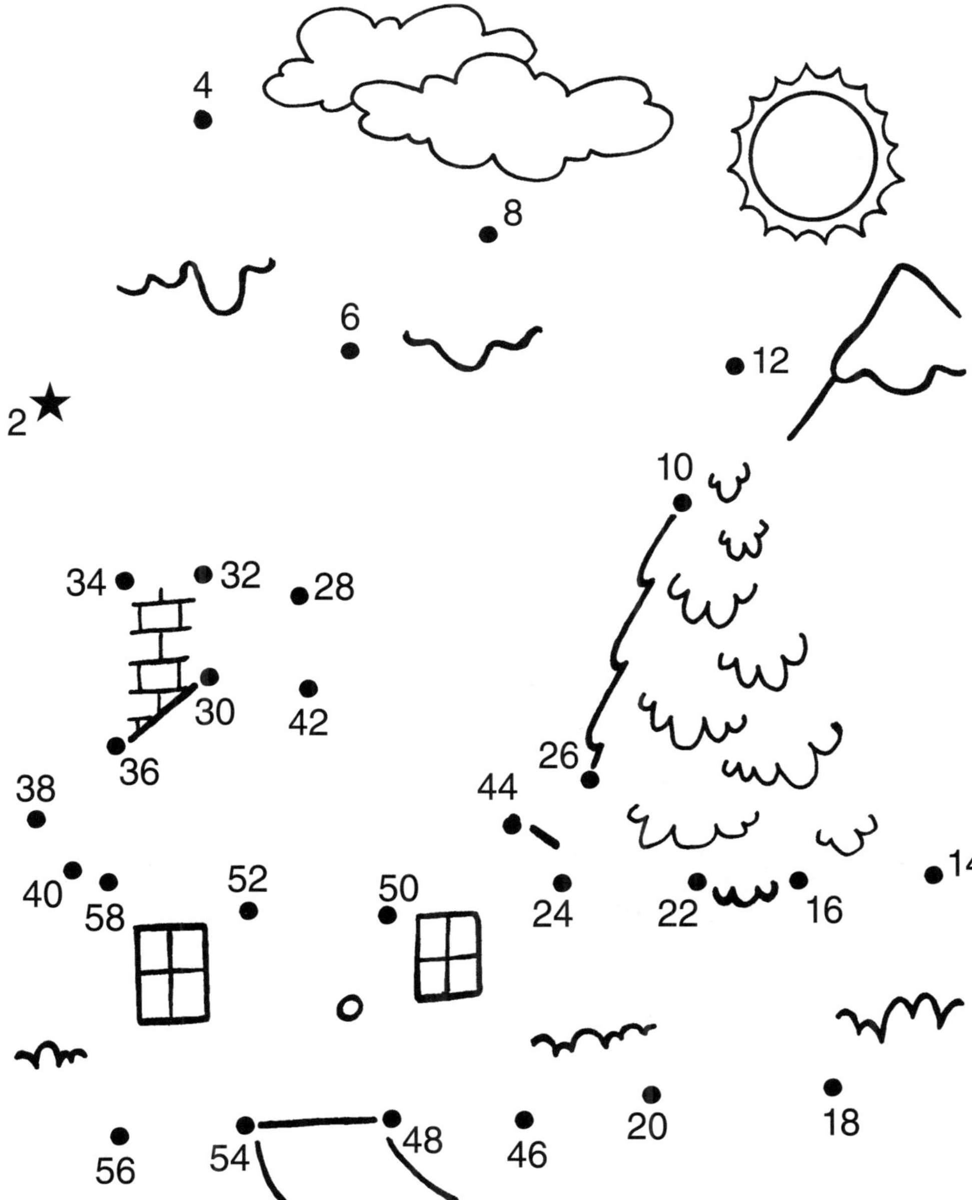

Seeing Double

Directions: Start at the number 2 and count by 2s to discover the hidden pictures. Do each of the puzzles separately.

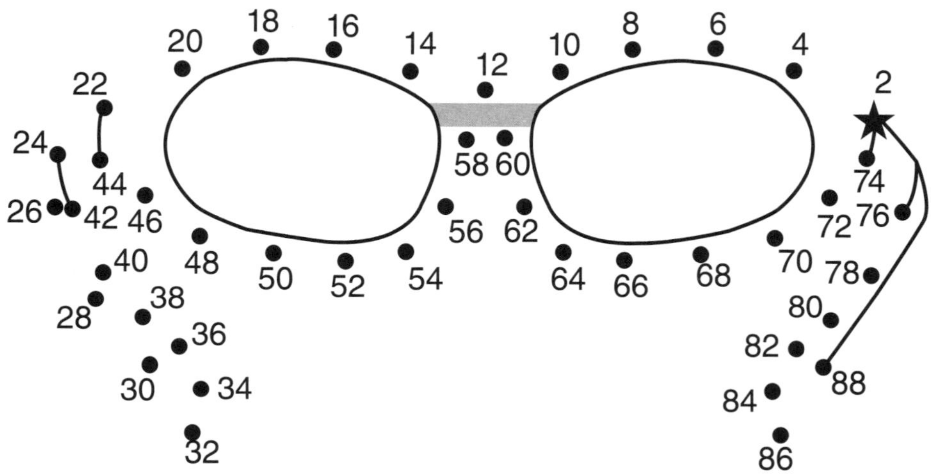

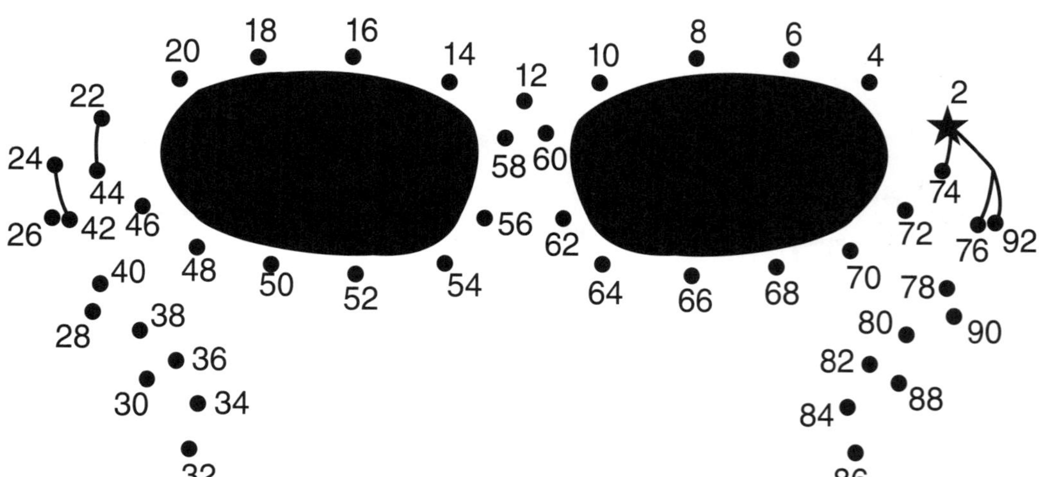

Follow the Dots

Directions: Follow the even numbers from 2 to 62 to complete the picture.

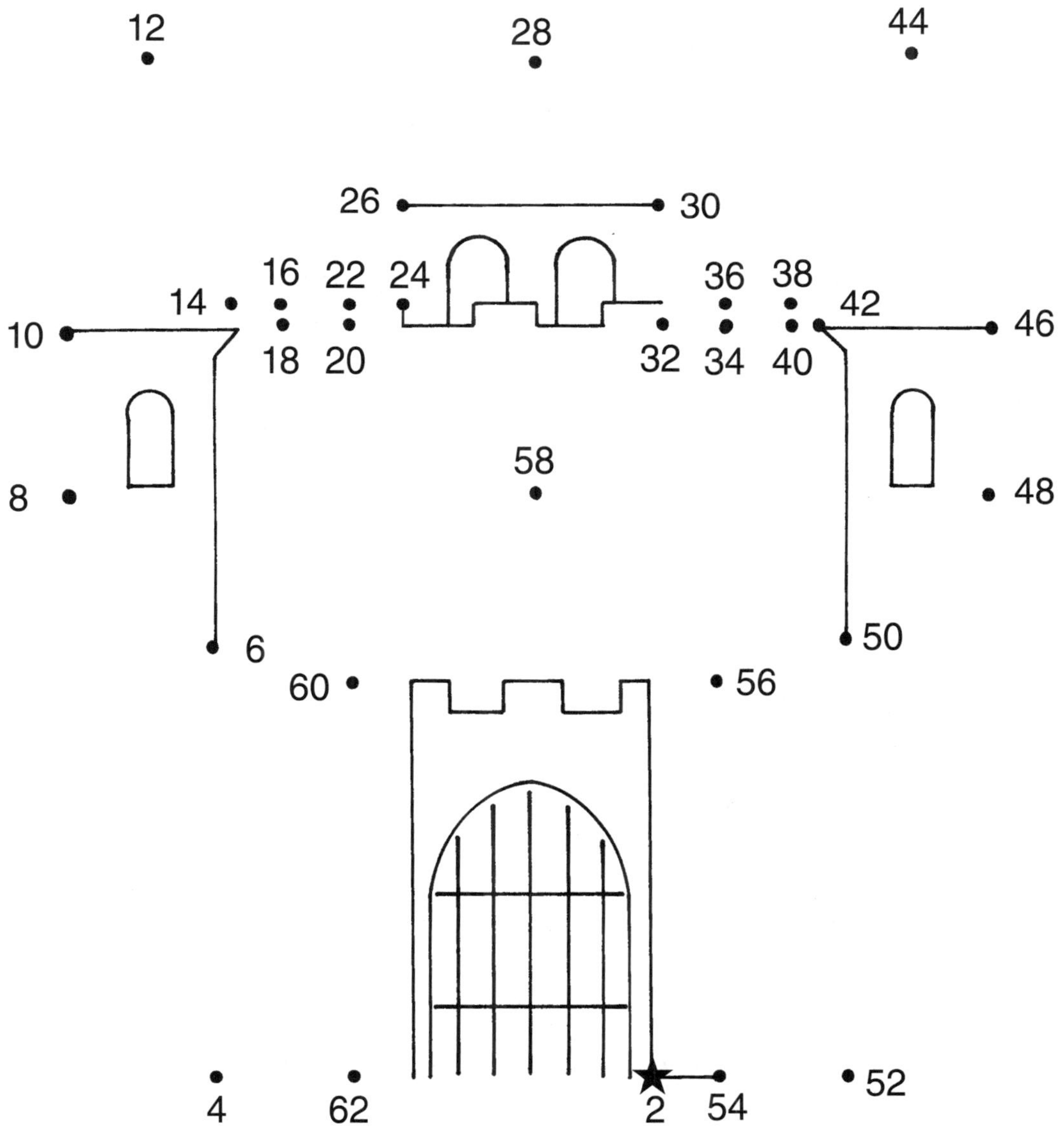

Count by 3s

Directions: To find who lives in the cactus, count by 3s and connect the dots.

Count by 5s

Directions: Count by 5s and connect the dots to complete the picture. Start at 0.

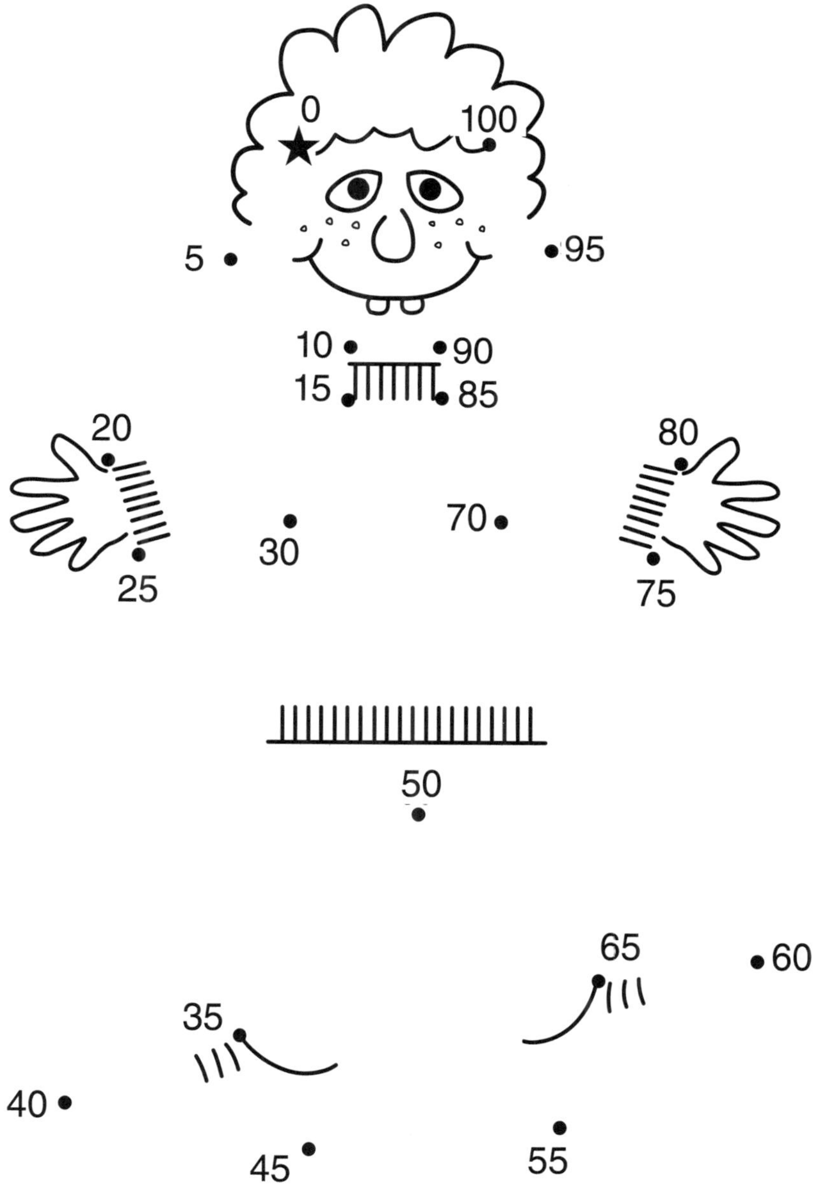

Bookworm

Directions: Count by 5s and connect the dots to complete the picture.

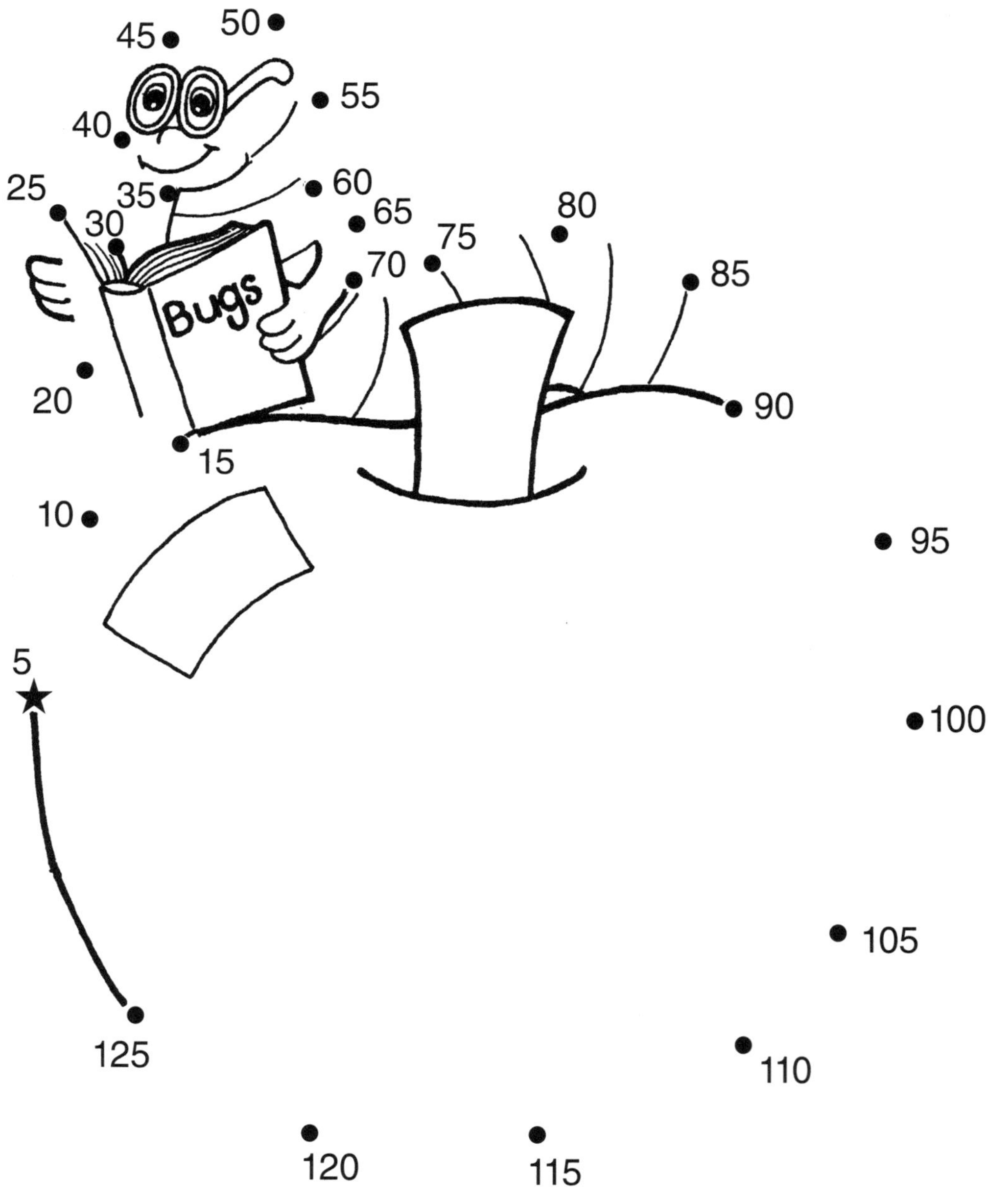

Counting by 10s

Directions: Count by 10s to fill in the blank lines. Then, complete the dot-to-dot, counting by 10s.

10, 20, ________, ________, 50

60, ________, ________, ________, 100

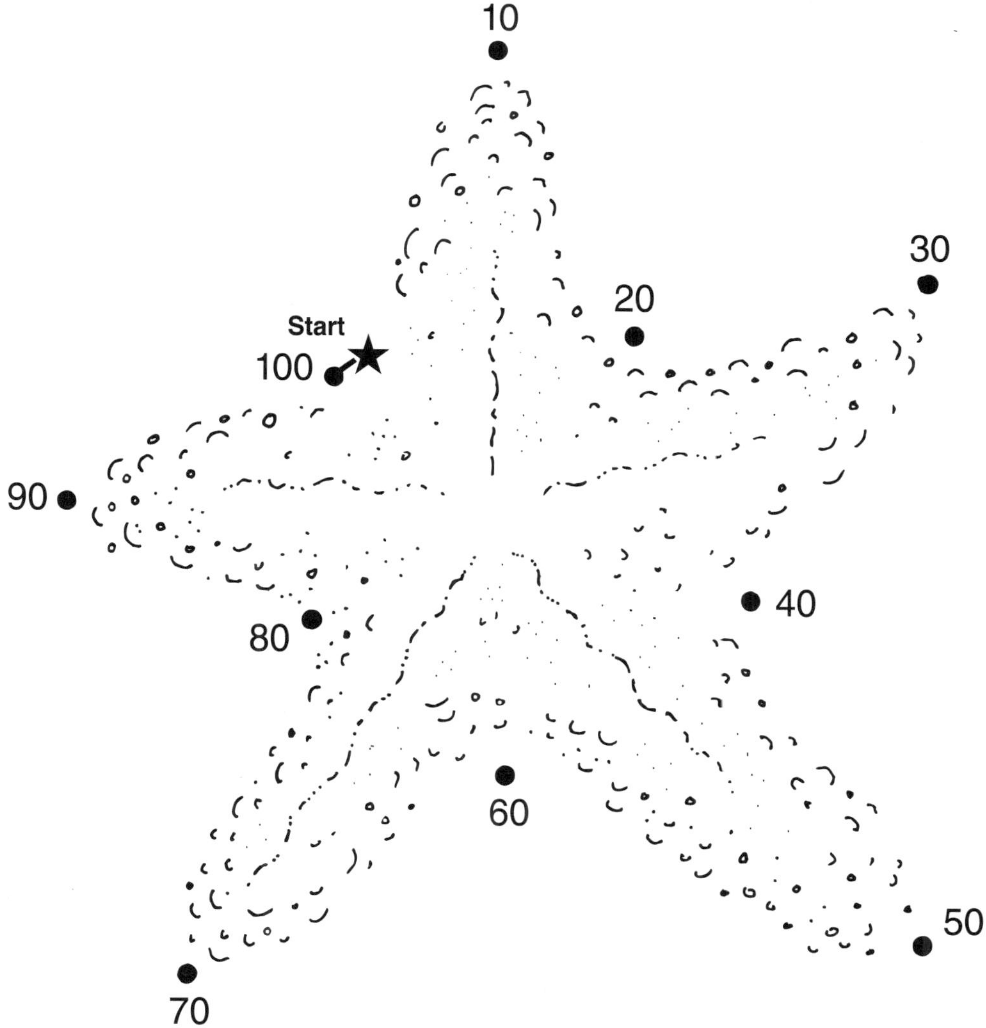

Hidden in the Lake

Directions: Here is a hidden picture. What do you think it might be? Starting at 0 and counting by 10s, join the numbers from 0 to 90 to complete the picture.

Counting in Hundreds

Directions: Count by 100s and connect the dots to complete the picture.

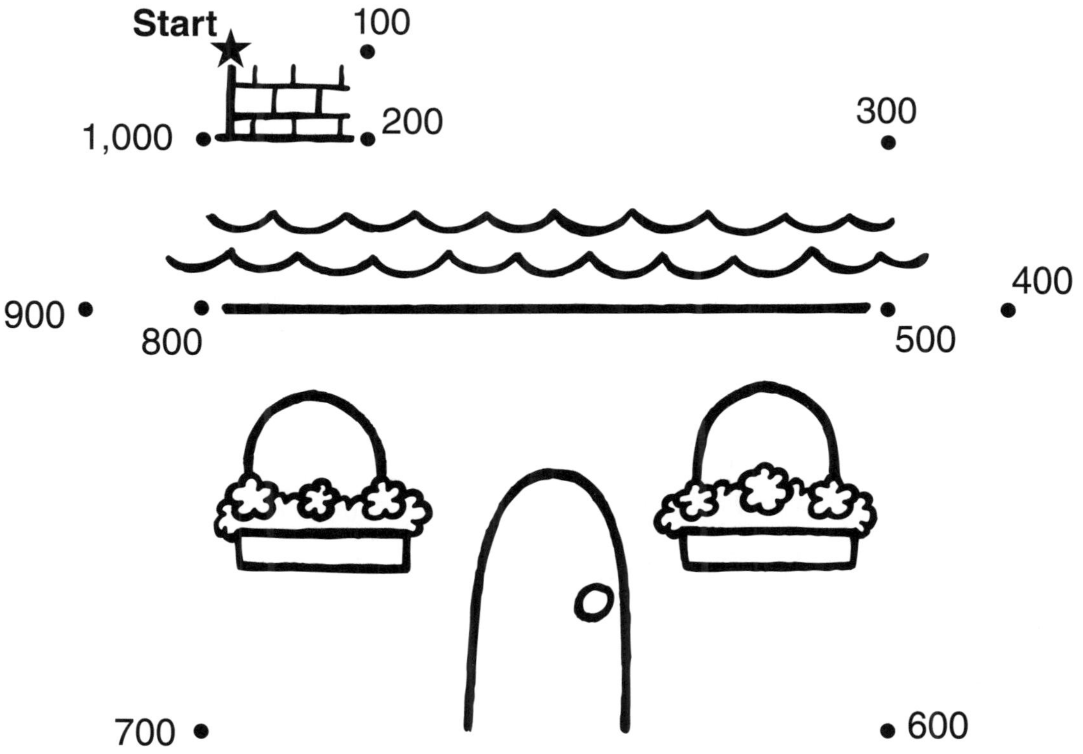

Fan

Directions: Start at "one." Read the number words to connect the dots to ten.

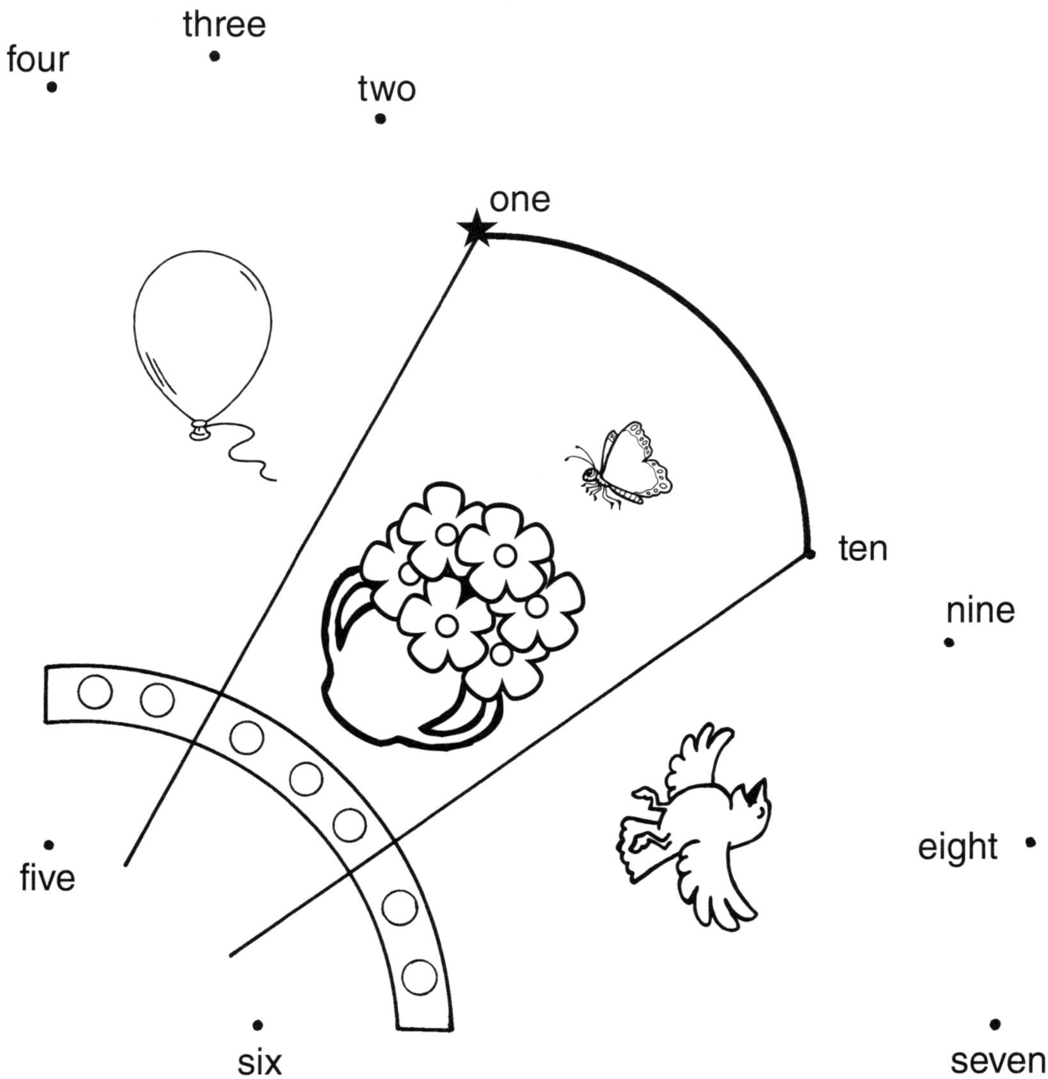

This Award Is Presented To

____

for

★ Doing Your Best

★ Trying Hard

★ Not Giving Up

★ Making a Great Effort